IMAGES
of America

TAMPA BAY
MUSIC ROOTS

ON THE COVER: The Outlaws were a Southern rock band that was formed in Tampa in 1969. The band became one of the first acts signed to Arista Records by Clive Davis in the mid-1970s. They would eventually become one of the most popular and successful Tampa Bay bands to ever get signed. (Courtesy of John Gellman.)

IMAGES of America
TAMPA BAY MUSIC ROOTS

Charlie Souza and Keith Wilkins
Foreword by Ronny Elliot

Copyright © 2020 by Charlie Souza and Keith Wilkins
ISBN 978-1-4671-0409-8

Published by Arcadia Publishing
Charleston, South Carolina

Library of Congress Control Number: 2019940808

For all general information, please contact Arcadia Publishing:
Telephone 843-853-2070
Fax 843-853-0044
E-mail sales@arcadiapublishing.com
For customer service and orders:
Toll-Free 1-888-313-2665

Visit us on the Internet at www.arcadiapublishing.com

I dedicate this book to two of my bandmates who have joined the great rock band in the sky: Buddy Pendergrass and Mel Dryer.

—Charlie Souza

I dedicate this book to the most important lady in my life— my daughter, Kayla. Daddy loves you always!

—Keith Wilkins

Contents

Foreword 6

Acknowledgments 7

Introduction 8

1. Birth of the Tampa Bay Music Scene: 1910s–1940s 11
2. Tampa Bay Discovers Rock 'n' Roll: 1950s 17
3. The Golden Age of the Tampa Bay Music Scene: 1960s 27
4. The Music Scene Plateaus: 1970s 53
5. The Music Scene Explosion: 1980s–1990s 65
6. The New Millennium: 2000s–2010s 91

FOREWORD

Oh, the stories we could tell. Fortunately, Charlie has told them so that we don't have to. As someone who has lived a life for rock 'n' roll and lived it in the Tampa Bay area, I could not be more grateful.

The big story starts, of course, with Elvis. Doesn't all history begin with Elvis? The Presley in Florida legend is well known and documented. His ties to the Tampa–St. Petersburg region are a major part of the entire Elvis Presley phenomena. No Elvis, no Beatles—and that's where our saga really begins.

In the 1950s and early 1960s, the Tampa Bay area had a healthy music scene. Of course, segregation meant that African Americans got the best of the deal with Charlie Brantley and His Original Honey Dippers and, later, the Skyliners. St. Pete and Tampa each had venues that figured prominently in the "chitlin' circuit," providing outlets for Ray Charles, Fats Domino, Hank Ballard, and most of the rest of the rhythm and blues stars of the day.

"Hillbilly" music flourished. Folk-music history was being made at Beaux Arts in Pinellas Park Dance orchestras, trying to keep up with the demise of swing, packed middle-class whites into Skyhaven, a dive bar in Tampa's Drew Park, trying to look like something else.

It was, of course, all becoming rock 'n' roll. We had Benny Joy, and we had the Arena Twins. It was all heading for the Impacs, the Rockers, the Dreamers, and Rodney and the Mystics. Tampa and St. Pete had a unique touch in those days, something vaguely Latin. Something special that would hang on overtime.

Where were we? Oh, yeah—the Beatles.

By 1964, everything had changed. Everything.

For a generation of us, our history of that era is written in the language of rock 'n' roll. Teen clubs were everywhere, in every neighborhood and every small town. Local bands had fan clubs. Records produced and recorded here were making their way around the globe. Every star came through Tampa or St. Pete, performing at Curtis Hixon Hall in Tampa, the Bayfront Center in St. Petersburg, Clearwater Auditorium, and the Lakeland Civic Center.

Young girls from junior high cherished an autograph from one of the Roemans as much as any precious jewel. Tropics records climbed the charts of the radio stations WLCY and WALT. The tiny, sweaty dance floor of the Surfers Club was holy. The Inn Crowd and the Spot forged their own legends. The world was ours. The music scene in this area from that period is based on magic as much as history.

Now, I'm not big on "glory days," and honestly, nostalgia bores me to death. I'd be lying to you, though, if I didn't admit that those were the best days of my life. In full disclosure, I should add that Charlie Souza taught me to play. Oh yeah, my first performance onstage was sitting in for him, too, at Madison Junior High School in Tampa in 1964. Charlie claimed to have the flu, and my pals in the Tropics were desperate. In fact, Charlie was performing with the Pastels. They were paying him more.

Thanks, pal.

—Ronny Elliot

ACKNOWLEDGMENTS

Charlie Souza and Keith Wilkins would like to thank the following individuals and organizations for their support as well as for their contributions to this book, which made it possible to put all these memories together: the Tampa Bay Music Scene Historical Society, the Florida Music Hall of Fame, the Tampa Bay Music Hall of Fame, Florida Magazine's Douglas Cifers, Bradley Davis of Noiz & Messiaxx, Ronny Elliot for agreeing to write the foreword for this book, everyone at Arcadia Publishing for allowing this book to happen, and Tedd Webb for all his support and for keeping historical records of all the great bands on his Tampa Bay Garage Bands website. Finally, thank you to all the musicians, fans, and Tampa Bay music scene professionals who submitted all of their photographs and stories for inclusion in this book. Thank you for helping to keep the memories alive!

Introduction

They say that music is the universal language, and this may very well be true. The simplest of melodies can make a sad person happy, turn stress into relaxation, and make the brokenhearted feel whole again. The industry behind the music, however, is a much more complex machine.

Before any music artist or band is lucky enough to make it to the big time, they all had to start somewhere. Look at any major city or metropolitan area in the United States, and you will find that each one has its own local independent music scene. Each of these music scenes has a countless number of aspiring artists and bands working hard to try and make a name for themselves in hopes of climbing out of the local music scene and becoming the next major worldwide act. Though very few of these acts will ever make the big time, a select few will at least make a major impact in their respective local music scenes—if they are lucky.

Florida has played an important part in the national music scene throughout the decades. Though Florida is divided up into several independent regional music scenes, Tampa Bay has always seemed to be the heart and soul, the nerve center of the state, giving birth to some amazing bands that had moved onto the national scene.

Tampa Bay's history as a professional music scene can be traced back to the 1910s. It was during that period in 1914 when the Peerless Quartet, though not actually from the Tampa Bay area, released the song "Way Down on Tampa Bay." Five years later, in 1919, the American Federation of Musicians–Florida Gulf Coast Chapter was formed.

Like many other local music scenes across the United States, Tampa Bay's music scene has seen major highs and lows throughout the decades. The scene went through one major boom in the 1960s. This period had seen countless local bands form and build huge followings. Bands such as the Tropics, the Tempests, the Impacs, the Satellites, Those Five, the Mystics, and countless others all made a huge impact in the 1960s.

As big as the 1960s was for the local scene, it paled in comparison to the huge boom that took place in the 1980s. At one point, during the late 1980s through the early 1990s, the bustling scene became so big that it received national attention, even being compared to the Los Angeles music scene. During this time, bands from all over the United States were relocating to Tampa Bay in the hopes of having a better chance of becoming noticed by record label executives and eventually getting signed to a record deal. Music venues were packed during this time. Recording studios, independent record labels, music attorney offices, and music magazines started opening up operations all over the Tampa Bay area as well. It was also during this period in the late 1980s when Tampa Bay became the epicenter of a new musical genre called death metal. Due to this, Tampa Bay earned itself the moniker of "the birthplace of death metal" by producing such acts as Death, Morbid Angel, Deicide, Obituary, Atheist, Hate Eternal, Monstrosity, Assück, Nocturnus, Acheron, and countless others. Morrisound Recording in Tampa played a huge part during this time by recording a huge majority of the death metal artists in their studios.

From blues to heavy metal, country to rock 'n' roll, and everything in between, Tampa Bay has always had a rich and diverse music scene. One does not have to look far to see Tampa Bay's contribution to music. Some of the acts to have gotten signed to major deals and who have gotten their start in Tampa Bay include the Outlaws, the Tropics, Savatage, Ray Charles, Stranger, Tampa

Red, Bertie Higgins, the Hazies, Roxx Gang, Julliet, Charlie Brantley, Iced Earth, and Kamelot. Many Tampa Bay acts have made a long-lasting impression in the area even though they never signed major deals. These acts include Diamond Gray, Arazmo, Messiaxx, Blackkout, Noiz, and Bleeding Hearts. Bleeding Hearts was such a hugely popular band in the early 1990s that its independent debut album, *Loaded Gun*, sold over 100,000 copies after its release in 1992. This was an impressive accomplishment for an unsigned local band, especially in a time before the Internet. Tampa Bay has been home to several legendary music venues that played a huge part in showcasing the local music scene throughout the years as well. Places like the original Cotton Club in Ybor City, the Clearwater Municipal Auditorium, the Surfer's Club in Madeira Beach, and the State Theatre in St. Petersburg, which still stands today.

There are a million stories that can be told about the Tampa Bay music scene—too many to cover in this book. Just ask any veteran of the scene, and they will tell you some typical stories about stages collapsing during a performance, a guitarist falling off the edge of the stage while giving a solo, and a singer suffering a heart attack in the middle of a show yet refusing to go to the hospital until the show was over. Those stories are all good, but how about the time in 1996 when the local band Eddie's Haircut held a CD release party and hired hair stylists to give $1 haircuts to their fans while the band performed? Or even the time that same year when Burdine's department stored aired television ads that featured several Tampa Bay bands modeling their fall fashion clothing to promote their "Back to School" sale?

The music business has changed considerably throughout the years. Due to the Internet and modern-day media technology, the record industry has all but died. Due to this, local music scenes all over the United States no longer thrive like they once did. Local artists no longer rely on local music scenes or record labels in order to get their names or their music out into the general public. During a time when music venues were constantly booked with original artists, nowadays they are booked with cover bands. For the younger generation, they will most likely never know what it was like to wait in line to get into a crowded club to hear their favorite local original band.

This book stands as a snapshot in time for the Tampa Bay music scene. It features major acts that got their start in Tampa Bay, as well as local artists and bands that, though they never quite made the big time, made a major impact on the local scene. This book is to stand as a testament to those acts, to forever acknowledge them for their contributions and possibly inspire future generations of aspiring musicians to live their dream and etch their own place in Tampa Bay music history.

One
BIRTH OF THE TAMPA BAY MUSIC SCENE
1910s–1940s

In 1919, the American Federation of Musicians–Florida Gulf Coast Chapter, a union for musicians that ensures proper compensation, was formed. Though many could consider this the birth of the Tampa Bay music scene, the scene itself did not really start to boom until the 1930s. During the 1930s and 1940s, there was a huge blues movement that formed in the Tampa/Ybor City area, specifically in the Central Avenue district.

Two of the biggest blues musicians who got their start in the Tampa area were Tampa Red, who grew up in the area known as "the Scrub," and Charlie Brantley. Brantley first learned how to play from a local musician known as "Piccolo" Pete. In 1944, Brantley formed a rhythm and blues band called Charlie Brantley and His Original Honey Dippers. The band became hugely popular in the Tampa Bay area and, eventually, throughout all of Florida as well. Brantley would eventually become a member of the Florida Collegians, a group of various professional musicians based in Tampa.

As blues music continued to gain popularity in the Tampa Bay area, so did the demand for venues that would showcase both local artists as well as national acts. One of the more popular venues in the area that featured live music regularly was the original Cotton Club. Located on Central Avenue, the Cotton Club was owned by the Joyner family. Other popular venues included Club Chiffon, Charlie Moon's Pool Hall, Johnny Gray's Bar, and the Blue Room, which was owned by Watt Sanderson.

Though blues was the most dominant genre in the 1940s, it was not the only genre to be found in the Tampa Bay area. The 1940s saw the formation of several symphony orchestras as well. This included the Tampa Symphony Orchestra, as well as several community and city orchestras in St. Petersburg.

One of the earliest examples of Tampa Bay's influence in music came in 1914 when the Peerless Quartet released their song "Way Down on Tampa Bay." Originally known as the Columbia Male Quartet, the vocal group was formed in New York by Columbia Records in the late 1890s. Around 1907, the group changed their name to the Peerless Quartet after releasing records for other record labels. The Peerless Quartet was the most commercially successful group during their time. The group recorded and released hundreds of recordings, including popular versions of songs such as "Sweet Adeline," "By the Light of the Silvery Moon," and "Let Me Call You Sweetheart." The Peerless Quartet is acknowledged as a major influence on the development of barbershop vocal harmony music. The group disbanded in 1928 and was inducted into the Vocal Group Hall of Fame in 2003. (Both, courtesy of University of Maine.)

Born Hudson Woodbridge in Smithville, Georgia, Tampa Red moved to Tampa following the death of his parents when he was a young boy. He grew up in the area of Tampa known as the Scrub, where he was raised by his aunt while learning how to master the slide guitar. (Both, courtesy of RCA Victor.)

Charles Brantley was born and raised in West Tampa during the turn of the 20th century. His career as a musician started in 1935, as a member of the Florida Collegians, a group of various Tampa musicians. Brantley was the founder of the Negro Musical Association and studied music through a correspondence course. Brantley was not only a master of the saxophone but also of every other major instrument of his day. (Courtesy of Douglas Cifers, FMI Publishing.)

Charles Brantley formed an R&B group, Charlie Brantley and His Original Honey Dippers, in 1944 at the age of 40. The band was the most sought-after R&B group of Florida in the late 1940s. Brantley had to quit performing with the band In June of 1949 due to a severe heart and nerve condition, though he still traveled with the band and handled their booking. In this image, Ray Charles is on the piano. (Courtesy of Douglas Cifers, FMI Publishing.)

Though born in Albany, Georgia, legendary singer-songwriter Ray Charles was raised in Greenville, Florida. After losing his eyesight at age seven, his mother sent him to the Florida School for the Deaf and Blind in St. Augustine. While there, Charles's musical talents started to surface. As a teenager, Charles moved to Tampa to live in a boardinghouse following the death of his mother. Charles soon joined the Tampa-based band Charlie Brantley and His Original Honey Dippers. In the late 1940s, Charles would move on to play in the Manzy Harris Orchestra. One of Charles's earliest recordings was "The St. Pete Florida Blues," a 1950 song Charles wrote about a girl he fell in love with in St. Petersburg. In 2019, the City of St. Petersburg declared February 15 "Ray Charles Day" during a special event that was held in the city. (Above, courtesy of Douglas Cifers, FMI Publishing; below, courtesy of Florida Department of State, Division of Cultural Affairs.)

Born in Vero Beach, Florida, in 1933, John Lamb started playing the tuba as a young boy. After graduating from high school, Lamb enlisted in the US Air Force and played in the military band. Following his service in the Air Force, Lamb switched to bass and joined Duke Ellington's orchestra in 1964. He would go on to tour with the band for three years. After moving to St. Petersburg in his later years, Lamb became a music teacher, teaching in various public schools as well as St. Petersburg College. Former students of Lamb include Stanley Clarke and Alphonso Johnson. Lamb was awarded the Jazz Club of Sarasota's Satchmo Award for his service to jazz. (Courtesy of Paul Wilborn.)

Jazz saxophonist Sil Austin was born Sylvester Austin in Dunnellon, Florida, on September 17, 1929. Austin taught himself how to play the saxophone at the young age of 12. In 1945, while still a teenager, Austin appeared on the *Original Amateur Hour* radio show, where he performed "Danny Boy." His performance ended up landing him a record deal with Mercury Records. Shortly after, Austin moved to New York, where he attended the Juilliard School of Music. Austin would eventually record over 30 albums for Mercury Records and had a number of Top 40 hits with such tunes as "Danny Boy," "Slow Walk" (which peaked at No. 17 on the charts), and "My Mother's Eyes." Austin left Mercury Records in the late 1960s and signed with SSS Records. Austin passed away on September 1, 2001, due to prostate cancer. (Courtesy of Douglas Cifers, FMI Publishing.)

Two

TAMPA BAY DISCOVERS ROCK 'N' ROLL

1950s

The 1950s started out fairly uneventful. It did see the formation of the St. Petersburg Symphony, which was formed by members of the Carreno Music Club of St. Petersburg. However, the once-thriving blues scene that dominated Tampa Bay during the 1940s started plateauing by this point. It would not be until a few years later, after the nationwide birth of rock 'n' roll, that the Tampa Bay music scene would start to grow again.

Once America came down with rock 'n' roll fever in the mid-1950s, Florida's own music scene started to grow tremendously. Eventually, Florida would become divided into numerous regional music scenes within the state. Five of these regions would stand out on their own to become the most dominate music scenes in the state. These regions were Gainesville, Jacksonville, Orlando, Miami, and Tampa Bay. Out of the five dominant music scenes, the Tampa Bay music scene was considered by many to be among the strongest of them all, giving birth to countless popular bands and artists.

Arguably the biggest act to form in Tampa Bay in the 1950s was the Arena Twins, formed by Sammy and Andy Arena. The Arena Twins hold a place in local music scene history as being the first-ever Tampa Bay musical act to be signed by a record company when they signed with Kapp Records in 1958. That same year saw the release of their single "Mama, Cara Mia" / "Little Pig."

The year 1959 would also see the formation of another local rock band, the Satellites. Formed in Plant City, the Satellites would eventually go on to have a huge following in the Tampa Bay area.

Also, in 1959, the Tampa Symphony Orchestra changed its name to the Tampa Philharmonic. This name change would be just one of several changes to come for the orchestra.

Born in Tampa and raised in Ybor City, twin brothers Sammy and Andy Arena started their musical career in 1959, billed as the Arena Twins. The Arena Twins got their start playing at local shows in Tampa before eventually touring all over the United States, where they played the finest ballrooms and performed in such places as the Mayfair Theatre, the Hudson Theatre, the Gaiety Theatre, and the Hillside Theatre. The group did a five-year stint performing in the Catskills, where they played at Kutchers Country Club, Grosinger's, the Raleigh Hotel, and many other hotels and resorts. The Arena Twins also spent five years performing in Miami at the Montmarte Hotel and did club dates at the Fountainbleau, the Doral Country Club, and most of the major hotels on Collins Avenue in Miami Beach. Eventually, the group moved on to Las Vegas, where they played the strip for many years and appeared with some of the biggest names in show business, such as Connie Frances, Buddy Hackett, Jose Ferrer, Anna Marie Albergetti, and Charlie Callis. (Courtesy of Douglas Cifers, FMI Publishing.)

The Arena Twins are considered to be the first-ever actual recording artists from Tampa Bay, first signing with Kapp Records and then later with Columbia Records in 1959. During their career, the group produced 14 records, all without ever having any formal musical training. Singles include "No One Else," "This Could Be the Night," "Jambalaya," "Judy Says," and "In My Wallet." (Courtesy of Douglas Cifers, FMI Publishing.)

Though born in Atlanta, Georgia, Benny Joy soon moved to the Tampa Bay area with his family. Joy started performing out on the local Tampa Bay club circuit, where he met another guitarist, Big John Taylor. The duo signed with TRI-DEC Records, where they recorded several demos including "Little Red Book," "Hey High School Baby," and "Miss Bobby Sox." Their first single was "Spin the Bottle," which was released in 1957. The song became a regional hit for Joy. In 1958, Joy signed with Ram Records and released his second single, "Ittie Bittie Everything." From 1958 to 1959, Joy toured Europe to support the Platters, Barry De Vorzon, Raymond Scott, and several others. During this time, Joy released his third single, "Crash the Party." The song was released on Decca Records in both the United States and Europe. (Both, courtesy of Douglas Cifers, FMI Publishing.)

Formed in 1955, the Tampa Skyliners was a direct descendant of the highly popular late 1940s–early 1950s Tampa-based R&B group Charlie Brantley and His Original Honey Dippers. Early pioneering Tampa Bay bands such as Rufus Beacham and his Tampa Toppers, as well as the Fabulous Rockers, were inspired by the Tampa Skyliners. (Courtesy of Douglas Cifers, FMI Publishing.)

Veteran blues singer-pianist Kitty Daniels was born in her parents' Eighth Avenue rooming house in Ybor City. She started performing publicly while attending Middleton High School in Tampa. After graduating from college, Daniels started taking gigs around Tampa. Eventually, Daniels joined Charlie Brantley and His Original Honey Dippers and then joined the Tampa Skyliners. Daniels has collaborated with Etta James, B.B. King, Dizzy Gillespie, and James Brown. (Courtesy of Kitty Daniels.)

The Fabulous Rockers formed by Dennis Pupello in 1957 and consisted of students attending Jefferson High School in Tampa. The band quickly became recognized as the most versatile group in the southeastern United States, performing six to seven nights a week. The band released two singles in 1961, "Stranger" and "Would I Still Be Loving You," the latter of which made the regional Top 40 chart and played on radio stations around Florida. After disbanding in 1963, the band reunited for a concert at the Tampa Convention Center in 1994, drawing a crowd of 6,000 concert goers. The Fabulous Rockers consisted of Dennis Pupello, Tony Lopez, Manuel Gutierrez, Onelio Ochoa, Donna Lynn Baccarella, Wes Young, Basil Rodriguez, Roger Menendez, Al Picallo, Roger Priede, Tony Raiano, Dave Jordan, Manuel Gutierrez, Chuck Borris, and Artie Alvarez. (Both, courtesy of Douglas Cifers, FMI Publishing.)

Bobby Lord was born on January 6, 1934, in Sanford, Florida, and grew up in Tampa. He attended Plant High School in his teen years and fine-tuned his rockabilly style of music while performing in numerous talent contests. Lord then started performing concerts at various Tampa dance halls, becoming hugely popular with the young crowd. After graduating from Plant High School, Lord enrolled at the University of Tampa. During his freshman year of school, he hosted his own hour-long television show called *The Bobby Lord Homefolks Show*. The show, which aired on WSUN-TV St. Petersburg on Saturday nights, featured Lord singing with a backup band. In 1952, Lord won a nationwide talent competition sponsored by *TV Guide*. Winning the competition led to him to appearing on Paul Whiteman's *TV Teen Club*, which aired on ABC-TV in Philadelphia. (Both, courtesy of Douglas Cifers, FMI Publishing.)

Lenny Dee was an organist whose records were among the most popular in the easy listening and space-age pop genres during the 1950s–1970s. His 1955 song "Plantation Boogie" charted in the top 20, and his 1969 album *Spinning Wheel* (Decca Records) went gold. Dee was offered his own television show in the mid-1950s called *Ladies' Day with Lenny Dee*. The show ran on WFLA-TV in Tampa. During the 1960s, Dee performed regularly at Davy Jones Locker, Desert Ranch Resort, and Dolphin Beach resort. In 1967, Dee opened his own club named Lenny Dee's Dolphin Den. Dee was a significant attraction in St. Pete Beach for decades. Dee spent the rest of his career in his nightclubs as well as touring. Dee retired in 2003 and passed away at his St. Petersburg home on February 12, 2006. (Both, courtesy of Douglas Cifers, FMI Publishing.)

Before becoming known as the manager who discovered artists such as Slim Whitman and Elvis Presley, "Colonel" Thomas Parker lived in Temple Terrace with his family during the 1940s and early 1950s. Parker worked as a field agent for the Hillsborough County Humane Society animal shelter on North Armenia Avenue. Aside from earning a stable wage, the job offered Parker and his family a rent-free apartment above the Humane Society, located in a remote part of West Tampa. Parker would use his experience as a promoter to raise money and awareness for the shelter, with some of his tactics being a little sketchy. Parker once gathered pups from three or four dogs and placed them with one mom. He then called *Tampa Tribune* reporter Paul Wilder with the scoop that one dog had 21 pups. Wilder, a respected journalist in his day, routinely fell for Parker's tricks. In 1956, Parker would give Wilder the first exclusive interview with Elvis Presley, no doubt payback for all the times Wilder fell for Parker's Humane Society publicity scams. (Courtesy of Tampa Bay Music Scene Historical Society.)

Tampa photographer William V. "Red" Robertson took this photograph of Elvis Presley at Tampa's Fort Homer Hesterly Armory on July 31, 1955. It was not the first time Presley had performed in Tampa. Presley had performed at the Fort Homer Hesterly Armory nearly three months prior on May 8 as the closing act in country singer Hank Snow's All Star Jamboree tour. Presley also performed at the Florida Theater in St. Petersburg one year later on August 7, 1956. (Courtesy of PictureLux, the Hollywood Archive, Alamy.)

Country and folk singer Slim Whitman was born in the Oak Park neighborhood of Tampa. Whitman worked various odd jobs at a Tampa shipyard while working on his musical career. He would perform with a variety of bands, including the Variety Rhythm Boys, the Light Crust Doughboys, and the Stardusters. Whitman's first big break came in 1948 when fellow Tampa Bay talent manager "Colonel" Thomas Parker heard Whitman singing on the radio and offered to represent him. That same year, Whitman signed with RCA Records and released his first single, "I'm Casting My Lasso Towards the Sky." During this time, Whitman kept his part-time job at the post office, as he was still unable to fully make a living from his music. That would soon change, as Whitman soon became a household name with a string of hits during the 1950s. (Both, courtesy of Douglas Cifers, FMI Publishing.)

Three

THE GOLDEN AGE OF THE TAMPA BAY MUSIC SCENE
1960s

The first major boom in the local music scene came in the 1960s, regarded by many as the golden age of the Tampa Bay music scene. The Arena Twins released two singles in 1960, "Jambalaya (On the Bayou)" / "This Could Be the Night" (Kapp Records) and "Notify the FBI" / "Oh, What A Shame" (Columbia Records).

The monthly "Star Spectacular" concert series was launched on August 16, 1961, at the Clearwater Municipal Auditorium. Conceived by Paul Cochran in conjunction with WLCY Radio, many local bands got their start at Star Spectacular, including Terry & the Pirates, the Fabulous Rockers, the Impacs, Rodney & the Mystics, the Roemans, and Vic Waters & the Entertainers. The Surfer's Club in Madeira Beach, owned by Margie and Dick Sexton, would become the springboard for countless area bands, one of which was the Tropics. Originally formed as a seven-piece horn band from Tampa, the Tropics dropped the horns, changed their line-up, and went for a more modern rock 'n' roll sound after being taken under the wing of the Sextons. The Tropics won the "International Battle of the Bands" competition, which took place on July 30, 1966, in Chicago, Illinois, beating out over 441 other bands from around the country. The victory landed the band a recording contract with Columbia Records.

The Tropics, along with other local bands, including the Outsiders and Those Five, appeared on the traveling music variety television show *Where the Action Is*, hosted by Dick Clark and filmed at the Bayfront Center Arena in St. Petersburg on December 11, 1965.

Other notable Tampa Bay acts of the 1960s included the Rovin' Flames, the Surprize, Blues Image, Blues Cycle, the Night Beats, and the Tempests. Upon forming in St. Petersburg in 1963, the members of the Tempests were only 13 years old.

Shortly after signing with Providence Records in 1966, the Soul Trippers had one of their songs pulled from several radio stations after it was discovered that the band consisted of five white men, not five black men, even though the single sold 20,000 copies.

On November 23, 1966, representatives from the St. Petersburg Symphony and the Tampa Philharmonic traveled by boat to the center of Tampa Bay, where they symbolically merged the two institutions to become the Florida Gulf Coast Symphony. The new symphony would have its first session on November 14, 1968. Then-43-year-old Irwin Hoffman was the music director.

The 1960s Tampa Bay band the Night Beats consisted of Joe Arkansas, J.D. Renney, Dave Barton, and Gary Myers. (Courtesy of Douglas Cifers, FMI Publishing.)

Originally formed in Ocala, the Royal Guardsmen helped to put Tampa on the map when they released their hit song "Snoopy Versus the Red Baron" in 1966. The song was recorded at Charles Fuller Productions on MacDill Avenue. Under the tutelage of producer Phil Gernhardt, the Royal Guardsmen went on to record and release several other hit songs throughout the late 1960s. (Courtesy of Bill DeYoung.)

Noah's Ark was a popular band from Tampa during the 1960s. The band consisted of Bobby Caldwell on drums, Buddy Richardson on lead guitar, Ronny Elliott on bass, Bill Mann on guitar, and, eventually, Rodney Justo on lead vocals. Caldwell previously played in the Go-Mads, and both Elliott and Richardson had previously played in other local bands, including the Ravens, the Outsiders, and the Soul Trippers. Caldwell would eventually leave the band to join Johnny Winter and, later, Captain Beyond. Richardson would eventually move on to form White Witch. Noah's Ark released two singles on Decca Records in 1967, including "I Get All the Luck" / "Love In" and "Paper Man" / "Please Don't Talk About Yesterday." Noah's Ark would later regroup as Duckbutter. (Both, courtesy of Ronny Elliot.)

Infinity's End was one of several Tampa Bay bands that Terry Bollea, popularly known as Hulk Hogan, performed bass guitar with during the late 1960s and early 1970s. Bollea was in ninth grade when he joined Infinity's End, and they quickly began performing at weekend parties. After Infinity's End, Bollea performed with the bands Koko and Ruckus, before going on to a career in professional wrestling. (Courtesy of Chet Yoakum, Tampa Bay Music Scene Historical Society.)

During his younger years, Stephen Stills of Buffalo Springfield and Crosby, Stills & Nash grew up in Tampa and attended Tampa's Plant High School. Stills also attended Admiral Farragut Academy in St. Petersburg and later attended the University of Florida. Pictured here are Crosby, Stills, and Nash at Criteria Recording Studios in Miami. (Courtesy of Joel Bernstein.)

Former Impacs lead singer Vic Waters formed Vic Waters and the Entertainers in 1966. Among the original 11 members that made up the band were Vic Waters, Jerry Michaels, Lance Abair, Gene Hilliard, Bobby Barnes, and Tom Saitta. Vic Waters and the Entertainers would pack local clubs. The band would play the Patio Lounge regularly, with thousands of kids showing up nightly to the show. The band released three singles on Crazy Horse Records in 1968, including "I'm White–I'm Alright," "Dreamer," and "The Greatest Love." In 1969, Vic Waters and the Entertainers signed with Capitol Records and released "Taking Inventory," an Eddie Floyd composition, which became a local hit in Florida and received a lot of national airplay as well. Pictured here are Vic Waters and the Entertainers with James Brown. (Both, courtesy of Lance Abair.)

Considered to be Florida's first music mogul, Phil Gernhard grew up in Sarasota and attended Sarasota High School. As a music producer based out of two offices in Tampa and St. Petersburg, Gernhard produced records for countless Tampa Bay bands during the 1960s, including the Tropics, the Ravens, Hoppi & the Beau Heems, and many more. Gernhard cowrote and produced the Royal Guardsmen's hit song "Snoopy Versus the Red Baron," which became the fastest-selling record of 1966. He also negotiated a record deal with Laurie records for the Royal Guardsmen. Gernhard produced Winter Haven natives Lobo ("Me and You and a Dog Named Boo") and produced "Let Your Love Flow," which was the first hit song for Pasco County's Bellamy Brothers. Gernhard also produced the hit song "Me and You and a Dog Named Boo" for Lobo. Gernhard has also cowritten or produced songs for other notable artists such as Dion, Hank Williams Jr., and William and the Zodiacs, just to name a few. (Courtesy of Billy Taylor.)

The Tropics were initially formed in 1963 as a six-piece R&B horn band, quickly gaining recognition in the Tampa Bay area. In 1964, Dick and Margie Sexton agreed to manage the band, providing the band dropped the horns, change their lineup, and change to a modern rock 'n' roll sound. The new lineup consisted of Mel Dryer (lead vocals), Eric Turner (guitar and vocals), Buddy Pendergrass (guitar and keys), Charlie Souza (bass and vocals), and Bobby Shea (drums). The Tropics played regularly at the Surfers Club, A teen dance hall owned by the Sextons in Madeira Beach. The Tropics released their first single, "I Want More," in 1965. The single, which became a number-one hit locally, was released on the Knight label with Freeport Records distributing nationally. Soon after, the band put on a show at Tampa's Curtis-Hixon Hall, which drew over 5,000 fans. (Above courtesy of Charlie Souza, Souzaphone Records Publishing, below courtesy of Douglas Cifers, FMI Publishing.)

The Ravens were formed in Pinellas County in 1965 by Brian Egan (bass and vocals), Mark Maconi (lead vocals), Rick Simpson (lead guitar and vocals), Richard "Thor" Simpson (rhythm guitar and vocals), and Paul Purcell (drums and vocals). The band started out being managed by Bob Orrick before eventually being managed by A.J. Perry. The band would rehearse in a seaside rental cottage managed by Purcell's parents before changing rehearsal space locations to Maconi's garage. Rick and Thor Simpson both left the band in 1966 and were replaced by Al Schweikert (lead guitar and vocals) and John Hallenstein (keyboards). The Ravens started out performing at frat parties and eventually moved up to nightclubs in Tampa and St. Pete. The band started opening for major acts that came to town, such as Roy Orbison, the Hollies, the Yardbirds, the Who, Herman's Hermits, Sonny and Cher, and many more. (Courtesy of Douglas Cifers, FMI Publishing.)

DANCE & HAVE FUN

At St. Petersburgs New

Outer Limits

Completely Air Conditioned

54th Avenue & 16th Street, North
(ACROSS FROM LI'L GENERAL)

Music By

RAVENS   JADES

Friday - 8 P. M. Till	$1.00
Saturday - 8 P. M. - 12:00	.75
Sunday - 2 P. M. - 5:00	.50
Wednesday - 7 P. M. - 10:00	.50

Girls free Sun. (Escorted)

The Ravens released their first single, "Reaching for the Sun" / "Things We Said Today," in the summer of 1966. The single was produced by Charles Fuller. The band would later perform both songs on a local teen television show that aired on WFLA. Egan left the band in 1967. The band released their second single in 1968, "Calamity Jane" / "Now She's Gone." As time went by, the Ravens would see various musicians come and go in the band including Ken Spivey (bass), Beau Fisher (bass), Al Schweikert (lead guitar and vocals), Chris Krawczyn (keyboards), Kent Pearson (bass), Tommy Angarano (organ and vocals), and Charlie Bailey (guitar). The Ravens single "Reaching for the Sun" / "Things We Said Today" would resurface once again on a 2001 compilation album titled *Psychedelic State: Florida in the 60s, Vol. 2*. (Both, courtesy of Douglas Cifers, FMI Publishing.)

KLWW NIFTY TOP 50

FOR WEEK ENDING APRIL 26, 1968

1 HONEY...BOBBY GOLDSBORO
2 FOGGY MOUNTAIN BREAKDOWN...FLATT & SCRUGGS
3 LOVE IS ALL AROUND...TROGGS
4 CALAMITY JANE...THE RAVEN
5 JENNIFER ECCLES...HOLLIES
6 VALLERI/TAPIOCA TUNDRA...MONKEES
7 YOUNG GIRL...UNION GAP
8 BONNIE & CLYDE...GEORGIE FAME
9 LADY MADONNA...BEATLES
10 UNICORN...IRISH ROVERS
11 QUESTION OF TEMPERATURE...BALLOON FARM
12 SUMMERTIME BLUES...BLUE CHEER
13 U.S. MALE...ELVIS PRESLEY
14 LEGEND OF XANADU...DAVE DEE & CO.
15 DR. JON...JON & ROBIN
16 MIGHTY QUINN...MANFRED MANN
17 THINK ABOUT YOU...NEW COLONY SIX
18 SOUL COAXING...RAYMOND LEFEVRE
19 SOUL SERENADE...WILLIE MITCHELL
20 BANANAS...GUY MARKS
21 RICE IS NICE...LEMON PIPERS
22 1941...TOM NORTHCOTT
23 UNKNOWN SOLDIER...DOORS
24 TAKE CARE OF MY BABY...BOBBY VINTON
25 BEAUTIFUL MORNING...RASCALS
26 CALL ME LIGHTNING...WHO
27 DELILAH...TOM JONES
28 LOUISIANA MAN...BOBBY GENTRY
29 SHOO-BE-DOO...STEVIE WONDER
30 SHERRY DON'T GO...LETTERMEN
31 GET TO KNOW YOU...SPANKY & OUR GANG
32 FOREVER CAME TODAY...SUPREMES
33 AIN'T NO WAY...ARETHA FRANKLIN
34 MONY MONY...TOMMY JAMES & SHONDELLS
35 ME THE PEACEFUL HEART...LULU
36 CINDERELLA ROCKAFELLA...ESTHER & ABI
37 DANCE TO THE MUSIC...SLY & FAMILY STONE
38 GOOD, BAD, UGLY...HUGO MONTENEGRO
39 CRY LIKE A BABY...BOXTOPS
40 GOODBYE BABY...BOYCE & HART
41 JUMBO...BEE GEES
42 PLACE IN MY HEART...DEAN MARTIN
43 LOOK TO YOUR SOUL...JOHNNY RIVERS
44 LOSING YOU...FRANK SINATRA
45 100 YEARS...NANCY SINATRA
46 RED RED WINE...NEIL DIAMOND
47 WAY TO SAN JOSE...DIONNE WARWICK
48 MASTER JACK...4 JACKS & A JILL
49 ANYTHING...ANIMALS
50 MY GIRL, HEY GIRL...BOBBY VEE

Tampa garage band Hoppi & the Beau Heems were initially formed in 1966 by Greg Hutchinson, Bob Orrick, and Bill Carson after being introduced to each other by Charles David Sheldon, owner of a popular mid-1960s teen nightclub called the Spot on Cypress Avenue. Hoppi Symons, Jim Eldridge, and Dickie Garrett joined the band soon after. Orrick and Eldridge would eventually be replaced by Lee Bailey and Steve Griggs. Hoppi & the Beau Heems released several singles on both the Gamma and Laurie record labels, including "I Missed My Cloud" (Laurie Records) in 1967, "When I Get Home" (Laurie Records) in 1968, and "Perdi Mi Nube" (Gamma Records) in 1968. (Both, courtesy of William Carson.)

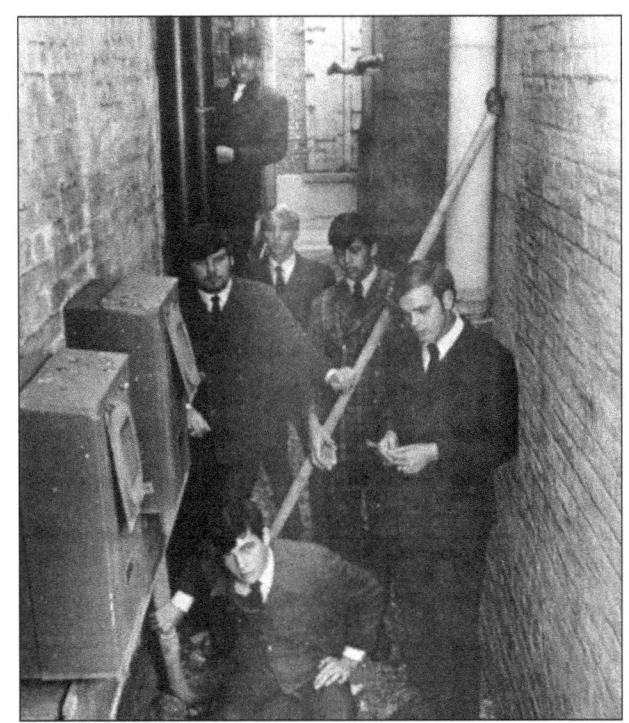

The Impacs were formed in St. Petersburg in 1960. Though the band members changed several times, the backbone of the band was Bobby Barnes (drums and vocals), Vic Waters (lead vocals), Jay Angello (guitar), Chuck Kaniss, (rhythm guitar and vocals), and Tony Brown (bass). The Impacs toured as part of Dick Clark's show, sharing the stage with big names such as Roy Orbison, Brenda Lee, Gene Pitney, or the Dovells. The Impacs recorded their first single, "I'm Gonna Make You Cry," for Cameo-Parkway Records in 1963. One year later, in 1964, the band signed with King Records and went on to release five singles and two LPs. The Impacs were the first band to play rock 'n' roll at the St. Petersburg Coliseum. (Both, courtesy of Lance Abair.)

Best known for their 1970 hit song "Ride Captain Ride," Blues Image was formed in Tampa in 1966 by guitarist Mike Pinera, drummer Manuel "Manny" Bertematti, percussionist Joe Lala, keyboardist Emilio Garcia, and bassist Malcolm Jones. After playing throughout Florida, Blues Image moved to Los Angeles, where they signed with Atco Records in 1959. Pinera left the band to join Iron Butterfly in the fall of 1969, during the recording of *Open*, and was replaced by singer Denny Correll and guitarist Kent Henry (formerly of Steppenwolf from 1971–1972). The band broke up after the release of their third album, *Red White & Blues Image*, in May 1970. Bertematti later played and recorded with New Cactus Band and toured with Iron Butterfly, Chi Coltrane, and Bobby Womack. Pinera also played with Iron Butterfly, New Cactus Band, Ramatam, and Alice Cooper. Konte joined Three Dog Night, and Lala played with Crosby, Stills, Nash & Young. Lala's percussion work also figures prominently on the Stephen Stills and Chris Hillman–led group Manassas. (Above, courtesy of Doug Cifers, FMI Publishing; below, courtesy of Michael Ochs.)

Formed in Tampa in 1964 as the Outsiders before changing their name in 1966, the Soul Trippers originally consisted of Hardy Dial on vocals, Buddy Richardson on guitar, Ronnie Vaskovsky on guitar, and Spencer Hinkle (the Tropics) on drums. Bassist Ronny Elliot (the Raveons) joined in 1965, and John Delise (Those Five Guys) eventually replaced Dial on vocals. In 1966, they were signed to Providence, a Laurie Records subsidiary label. (Courtesy of Ronnie Elliot.)

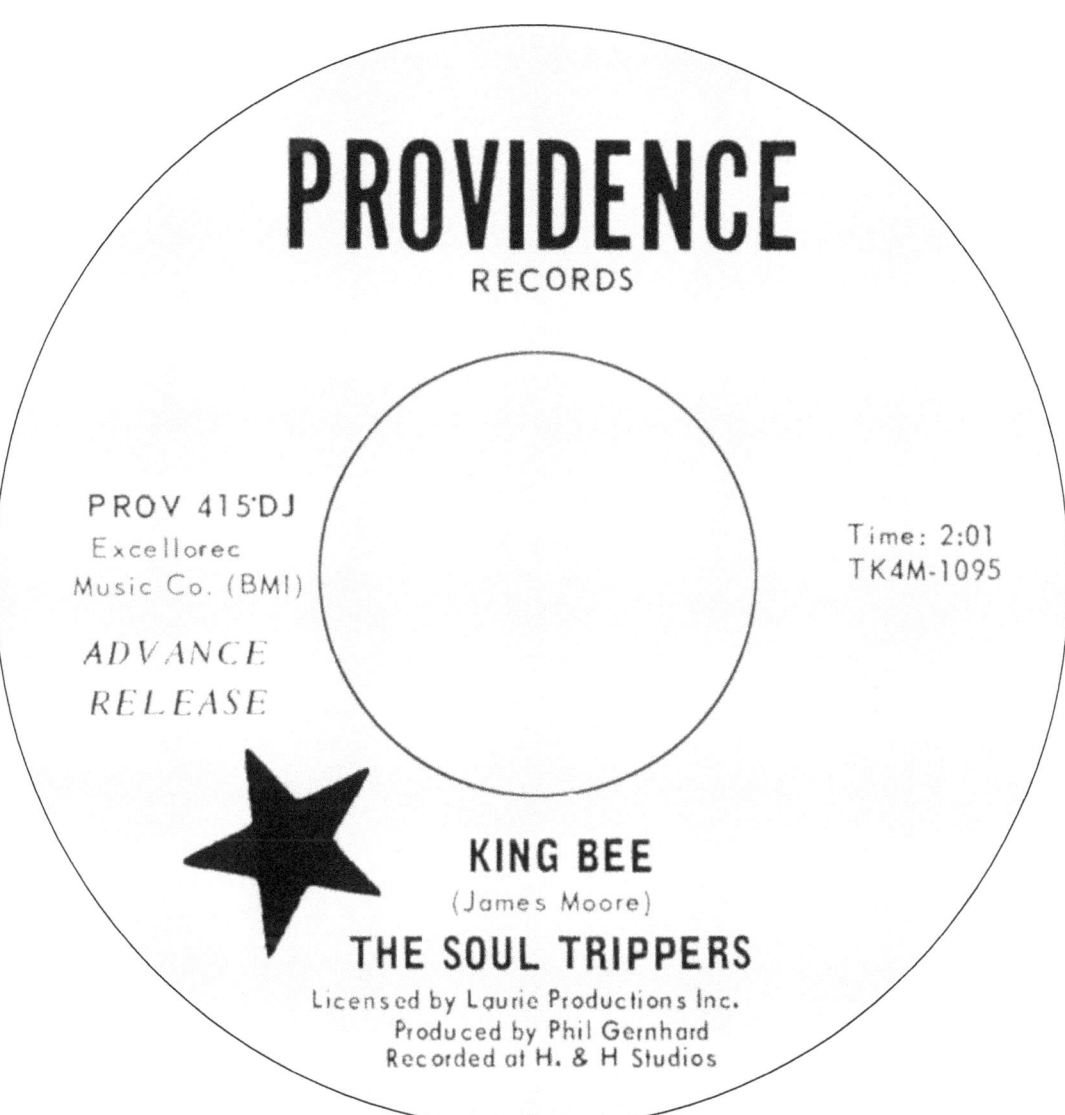

As the Outsiders, the Soul Trippers released their first 45, "She's Coming on Stronger," at Tampa's H & H Avenue and, later, a cover of Eddie Cochran's "Summertime Blues." They released a cover of James Moore's "(I'm a) King Bee," which sold 20,000 copies before the discovery that the band consisted of five white guys, which resulted in it getting pulled from radio station playlists. This act of reverse racism led to the band splitting up. (Courtesy of Ronnie Elliot.)

The SPLIT ENDS

Paul E. Deutekom
PERSONAL MANAGER
ST. PETERSBURG
4641 - 66th Street North
Tel: 544-6009

Boot originally formed in 1963 as the Allusions. A few years later, the band changed their name to the Split Ends and released their single, "Rich With Nothing" / "Endless Sea." A few years later, the band changed their name to Boot. As Boot, the band released two albums, including their self-titled album, followed by *Turn the Other Cheek*. Boot performed on the Dick Clark Tour *Happening '67* and the Dick Clark band contest show *Happening '68*. Over the years, Boot performed with many big acts, including Canned Heat, Jefferson Airplane, Iron Butterfly, Steppenwolf, B.B. King, Neil Diamond, the Allman Brothers, Lynyrd Skynyrd, and many more. Following their breakup, Bruce Knox died of pancreatic cancer, Dann Eliassen went on to play with some Beatles cover groups, and Jim O'Brock became an accountant and company pilot for Louisa Health Resorts. (Courtesy of Douglas Cifers, FMI Publishing.)

The Roemans, originally spelled the Romans, were another hugely popular Tampa Bay band in the 1960s. The members of the Roemans were slightly older than most of the other bands in the local scene at the time. The Roemans appeared as the backup band for Tommy Roe on his 1964 recording "I Think I Love You" / "Oh So Right" (ABC Paramount Records), as well as Roe's 1965 recording "Diane from Manchester Square" / "Love Me, Love Me" (ABC Paramount Records). The Roemans were signed to ABC Paramount Records following a performance of theirs at the Bradenton Auditorium. Prior to the show, the band's manager had informed them that there were going to be some important A&R men in attendance and that they needed to make a good impression. To help accomplish this, the band filled the front rows with approximately 300 girls from their fan club who would continuously cheer, scream, and even faint during the performance. (Courtesy of Douglas Cifers, FMI Publishing.)

Between 1964 and 1966, the Roemans released six singles on ABC Paramount Records including "Give Me a Chance" / "Your Friend," "Misirlou" / "Don't," "Universal Soldier" / "Lost Little Girl", "Listen To Me" / "You Make Me Feel Good," "When the Sun Shines in the Mornin'" / "Love (That's All I Want)," and "All the Good Things" / "Pleasing You Pleases Me." Their singles received regular airplay locally. In 1966, the Roemans toured the United Kingdom with singer-songwriter P.J. Proby. While on tour, the band was approached by Beatles producer Brian Epstein. Impressed with the Roemans, Epstein wanted to sign the band. However, the deal was declined by the band's American management. Eventually, the Roemans' drummer, Bertie Higgins, would go out on his own as a solo artist and find success with his 1981 hit song "Key Largo." (Both, courtesy of Douglas Cifers, FMI Publishing.)

The Saltwater band was a 1970s Tampa Bay rock band that formed in Treasure Island. Posing in this 1977 band photograph are, from left to right, Tom Gribbin, Kathy Shoemaker, Bob Shoemaker, Marc Huepenbecker, and Bill DeYoung. Eventually, the band would change its name to Tom Gribbin & the Saltwater Cowboys. (Courtesy of Bill DeYoung.)

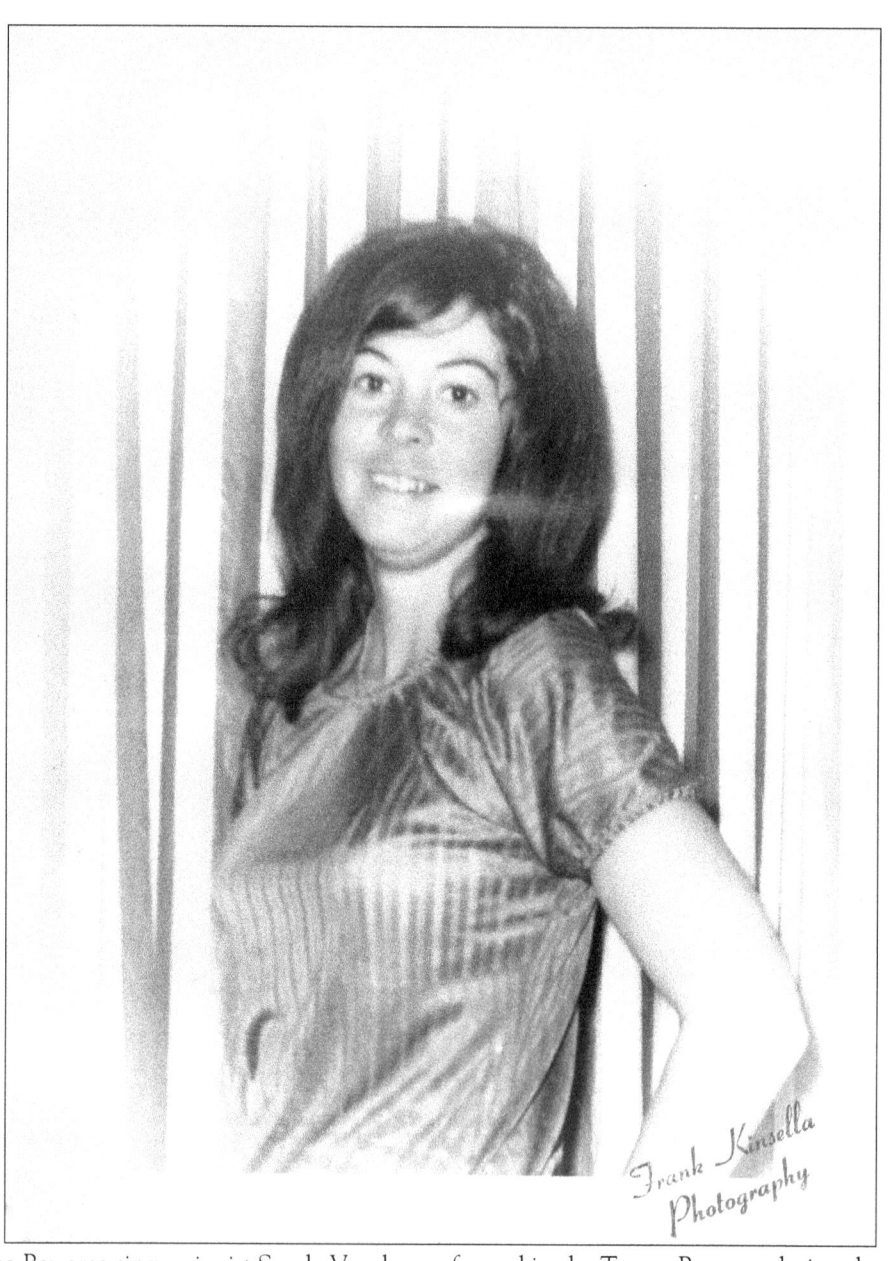

Tampa Bay area singer-pianist Sandy Vaughn performed in the Tampa Bay area during the mid- to late 1960s. Sandy is originally from Marietta, Ohio, where her mother owned and operated a dancing school there since 1947. In 1959, Sandy and her family moved to Tampa, where she took piano and French horn lessons and was in the marching band at Tampa's Wilson Junior High. She attended Plant High School until her senior year and then moved to Daytona Beach briefly before returning to Tampa in 1967. Sandy performed regularly at Gay 90s, which was located on Gandy Boulevard, just east of McDill Avenue. Sandy would briefly play with Rockin' Ricky and the Routiners, who would do shows at the Men's Garden Club, which is now where the International Mall is located. Though she had been performing on stage since the age of three, Sandy decided to leave the music business in 1969 and move to Micanopy, Florida, to manage an antique business. (Courtesy of Sandra McCann.)

The Movers were a rock band formed locally in Port Richey. The band consisted of Bobby Langford, Roger Hale, Don Reynolds, Carlton Sumner, Steve Uzzle, Butch Calkins, and Bob Goluba. The Movers signed with Capitol Records and released their first single, "Birmingham" / "Leave Me Loose," in 1968. Later that same year, the Movers would release their second single, "Hello L.A. (Bye Bye Birmingham)" / "Hey You, Hey Me." (Courtesy of Douglas Cifers, FMI Publishing.)

The Travelers were a Tampa Bay band consisting of, from left to right, Stan Powell, Dale Hadley, Cheryl Cooper, Mark Bass, Bonnie McCartney, Bob Carter, and Bill Mathis. The Travelers played hundreds of gigs, were the official group of the Festival of States and were featured in local newspapers often. This photograph was taken at the St. Pete Yacht Club ballroom for the Jr. Sungoddess announcement ceremony. (Courtesy of Bob Carter.)

On May 6, 1965, the Rolling Stones performed a show at Jack Russell Stadium in Clearwater, appearing on the bill with several local bands. The Stones' set was cut short, however, due to a large group of teenagers who were screaming and attempting to rush the stage. The band members were escorted to an awaiting white station wagon and driven away from the stadium while being chased by a mob of teenagers. They were taken to the Jack Tar Harrison Hotel (now called the Harrison Hotel) in downtown Clearwater where they were staying. Later that night, while trying to sleep in his room, Keith Richards woke up with an idea for a guitar riff. Richards grabbed his guitar and played the riff into a tape recorder. Several days later, the band entered Chess Recording Studios in Chicago and recorded "(I Can't Get No) Satisfaction," based on the riff that Richards came up with back at the hotel in Clearwater. The song was released the next month in June, eventually becoming the signature song of the Rolling Stones. (Courtesy of WFLA, the *St. Petersburg Times*, Francis Brush.)

Tampa Bay band Bee's Knees was the youngest local rock band to play the Florida circuit during their time. The band featured 13-year-old guitarist Richard Kruzell, his older brother Roger Kruzell on bass, Ricky White on rhythm guitar, Mike Swisshelm on drums, Doug Johnson on drums, and Bob King on lead vocals (later replaced by Herbie Fluit, then known as Joe Yovino). The band performed at countless civic centers, as well as other places such as the Northgate Shopping Center, the Purple Underground, the Hullabaloo, the Sacred Heart, the Inn Crowd, the Tigers Den, Lake Ellen Beach (pictured here), Lowry Park, Tampa Stadium, and the fairgrounds. Richard Kruzell would eventually go on to play with Tampa Bay band White Rock, fill in with White Witch, and tour with Tampa Bay rock legend Mike Pinera and the Image. Richard is the current world record holder for playing the most solo shows during Spring Break in Fort Lauderdale—319 shows in one season. Richard studied songwriting and music business in Nashville, Tennessee, and still performs around the Tampa Bay area. (Courtesy of Richard Kruzell.)

Jazz saxophonist "Cannonball" Adderley was born in Tampa on September 15, 1928. Adderley moved to Tallahassee with his parents after they both accepted teaching jobs at Florida A&M University. Adderley teamed up with his brother Nat and played with Ray Charles when Charles lived in Tallahassee during the early 1940s. After finishing his music studies at Florida A&M in 1948, Adderley moved to Broward County and became the band director at Dillard High School in Fort Lauderdale. Adderley stayed on as the school's band director until 1950. Adderley released his soul-jazz single "Mercy, Mercy, Mercy" in 1966. The single was a crossover hit on the pop charts and was eventually covered by the Buckinghams. Adderley worked with trumpeter Miles Davis on his records *Somethin' Else* (1958), *Milestones* (1958), and *Kind of Blue* (1959). (Both, courtesy of Devon "Doc" Wendell.)

The Doors lead singer, Jim Morrison, spent the first three years of his life in Clearwater with his parents. After moving away briefly, Morrison returned to Clearwater to live with his grandparents off of Druid Road. At age 18, Morrison entered St. Petersburg Junior College (SPJC) to study philosophy and psychology. After his first year at SPJC, Morrison moved to California briefly before returning to Clearwater to finish his second year at SPJC. Morrison frequently took the Trailways Bus across the causeway, getting off at the downtown terminal and walking west along Lafayette Street (now Kennedy Boulevard) to visit the House of Seven Sorrows Café, just west of the Hillsborough River at Parker Street. Morrison was also a regular at Beaux Arts in Pinellas Park, located on Sixtieth Street near Seventy-Seventh Avenue. While there, Morrison would often read his poetry to visitors on occasion. Morrison would often hitch rides to Clearwater Beach to walk along the shore all night. After graduating from SPJC with a "C" average, Morrison attended Florida State University. (Photograph by Joel Brodksy, courtesy of Gene Lee, Rhino Entertainment Company.)

Born in Florida, Iron Butterfly and Captain Beyond guitarist Larry "Rhyno" Reinhardt started his career in the 1960s playing in the Bradenton-Sarasota music scene. Reinhardt played in several local bands, including the Thunderbeats, as well as a psychedelic blues-rock power trio called the Load, which also featured bassist Richard Price and drummer Ramone Sotolongo. Reinhardt also played in a local band called the Second Coming, which also included Dickey Betts (guitar), Dale Betts (vocals and keyboards), Berry Oakley (bass), John Meeks (drums), and Reese Wynans (keyboards). Dicky Betts and Berry Oakley would eventually go on to join the Allman Brothers Band. Reinhardt joined Iron Butterfly in 1969. One year later, fellow Tampa musician Mike Pinera (Blues Image) also joined Iron Butterfly. Both Reinhardt and Pinera appear on Iron Butterfly's 1970 album, *Metamorphosis*. Reinhardt, along with Iron Butterfly bassist Lee Dorman, formed Captain Beyond in 1971, signing with Capricorn Records. (Courtesy of Mark T. Kracker.)

Four

THE MUSIC SCENE PLATEAUS
1970s

The local music scene in the 1970s changed as people's tastes in musical styles changed. Due to this, most of the bands that had gained prominence in the Tampa Bay area during the 1960s eventually started disbanding in the 1970s. However, the 1970s would see its fair share of popular Tampa Bay bands as well. Bands like Southern Mother Trucking Company, the Hats, Rich Rag$, Boot, Buckwheat, and the Sugar Beats all had a huge fan base.

One of the more short-lived but popular bands of the time was Bacchus. Formed after the breakup of the Tropics in 1969, the band featured former Tropics members. Bacchus would play a lot of memorable shows at Lowrey Park in Tampa. The band would break up in 1973.

Another band that quickly rose to popularity in the 1970s was Just Boys. Formed in Tampa in 1976, Just Boys was a melodic rock band that was labeled by many as punk, new wave, and even power-pop at times.

One of the biggest Tampa Bay bands of the time was the Outlaws. Though originally formed in Tampa in 1967, the band rose to prominence in the 1970s. The Outlaws became the very first act to be signed to Arista Records under Clive Davis.

A young bass guitarist named Terry Eugene Bollea started making a name for himself in the 1970s while playing in several popular Tampa Bay bands, including Infinity's End, Koco, and Ruckus. However, it would be the world of professional wrestling that would make Terry Eugene Bollea a household name, once he changed it to Hulk Hogan.

In 1978, two brothers named Chris and Jon Oliva formed their first band together, Avatar, from the ashes of their former bands Tower and Alien, respectively. Due to legal reasons, however, Avatar would eventually have to change their band name. The new band name that Avatar would settle on was Savatage, and they would eventually go on to take the Tampa Bay area by storm in the 1980s and help usher in the explosion that was the 1980s Tampa Bay music scene.

Formed in Tampa in 1967 by guitarists-vocalists Frank Guidry, the Outlaws would become one of the most popular and most successful Tampa Bay bands to ever get signed. The band became one of the first acts signed by Clive Davis to his then-fledgling Arista Records. The band's first three albums, *The Outlaws*, *Lady in Waiting*, and *Hurry Sundown*, featured radio-favorite songs such as "There Goes Another Love Song," "Green Grass & High Tides," "Knoxville Girl," and "Freeborn Man." All would become worldwide gold and platinum landmarks. The Outlaws toured with such bands as the Allman Brothers, Lynyrd Skynyrd, the Marshall Tucker Band, and the Charlie Daniels Band, the Doobie Brothers, the Who, Eagles, and the Rolling Stones. Over the next 20-plus years, the Outlaws would experience rampant personnel changes, ill-fated reunions, and bitter trademark battles. (Both, courtesy of Douglas Cifers, FMI Publishing.)

White Witch formed in 1971 in Tampa, originally consisting of Ron Goedert (lead vocals), Charles "Buddy" Richardson (guitars), Buddy Pendergrass (keyboards), Beau Fisher (bass), and Bobby Shea (drums). Though primarily known as a glam rock band, White Witch's music encompassed various genres, including progressive rock, psychedelic rock, hard rock, honky-tonk, Southern boogie, and pop-rock. Their song lyrics had a new age/spiritual theme that ran through them. After touring small venues around the Southeast for the first year, White Witch signed with Capricorn Records. Though the band was a little uneasy about being the only non-Southern rock band signed to the label, White Witch agreed to the contract without having a manager or legal representation look it over first. The band quickly recorded their self-titled debut album in Capricorn's Macon, Georgia, recording studios. (Both, courtesy of Souzaphone Records Publishing.)

White Witch toured extensively to support their debut album, opening for such artists as Alice Cooper, Grand Funk Railroad, and Billy Preston. Fisher left the group after the album's release and was replaced by Rabbi Barbee, who eventually left himself in 1974. Bassist Charlie Souza and drummer Bill Peterson soon joined the band. Due to displeasure with their record company, Buddy Richardson left the group immediately after their second album, *A Spiritual Greeting*, was completed. Richardson was replaced by guitarist George Brawley. Though the band toured briefly after this, White Witch broke up shortly after in 1975. Following the breakup, Goedert recorded and released some solo recordings, Pendergrass got work as a commercial jingle writer and opened his own recording studio, and both Richardson and Souza went on to play in other bands. (Both, courtesy of Charlie Souza, Souzaphone Records Publishing.)

"Marvelous" Marvin Boone is a veteran disc jockey whose voice has graced Tampa Bay's airways on such stations as Mix 96, 1040 WHBO AM, WFLA, WGUL, WGHR Hits 106, and Q-105. Hailing from New Port Richey, Boone started out as a drummer before getting into radio. After performing in numerous bands, Boone decided to go to broadcasting school. Boone got his start in radio in 1977 at Tampa's WGUL AM & FM, where he was given his own "oldies" radio show on Saturday nights, *Old Gold Retold*. Boone's radio show became hugely popular, staying on the air for 10 years. Eventually, Boone moved on and went to work for Q-105 to host his top-rated lunchtime request show, *The Bouffant Buffet*, which stayed on the air for nearly 20 years. In 2009, Boone moved over to WGHR Hits 106. (Both, courtesy of Marvin Boone, WGHR Hits 106.)

Tampa Bay veteran disc jockey "Marvelous" Marvin Boone was given his nickname by the late radio legend Scott Robbins. Though Boone does not know how Robbins came up with the name for him, the nickname caught on with listeners. Outside of being a disc jockey and drummer, Boone is also a songwriter, as well as the vice president of the local chapter of the Buster Keaton Fan Club. (Courtesy of Marvin Boone, WGHR Hits 106.)

Country legends David and Homer Bellamy, better known as the Bellamy Brothers, grew up in Darby, Florida. David and Homer's father was a member of a Tampa Bay–area Western swing band. In 1968, the two brothers performed their first gig with their father at the Rattlesnake Roundup benefit concert held in San Antonio, Florida. The annual event still takes place to this day, though it is now called the Rattlesnake Festival. Following their first gig at the Rattlesnake Roundup, the Bellamy brothers started performing at various fraternity parties at the University of Florida. Eventually, the brothers moved to Atlanta and formed a band called Jericho, though they soon moved back home to Tampa Bay. The Bellamy Brothers signed to Curb Records in 1975 and went on to become huge country stars throughout the 1970s and 1980s. (Both, courtesy of Douglas Cifers, FMI Publishing.)

Best known for his 1981 hit "Key Largo," Bertie Higgins grew up in Tarpon Springs, Florida. Higgins began his career in show business at the age of 12 as a ventriloquist. It was here where he competed and won many local talent contests, becoming a favorite at school assemblies all around the Tampa Bay area. (Courtesy of Douglas Cifers, FMI Publishing.)

Higgins's first band would perform all over the Tampa Bay area, where they would play proms, homecoming dances, and sock hops. After graduating from Tarpon Springs High School, Higgins studied journalism and fine art at St. Petersburg College. After leaving college, Higgins joined the Tommy Roe band and the Roemans as their drummer, touring with groups such as the Rolling Stones and the Beach Boys. (Courtesy of Douglas Cifers, FMI Publishing.)

Higgins eventually left the Roemans and returned home to Florida, where he started perfecting his songwriting abilities. Higgins would eventually become in high demand and start performing in venues throughout Florida. During this time, he became a protégé of actor-director Burt Reynolds, who recognized Higgins's writing potential. Reynolds would go on to tutor Higgins in screenwriting. (Courtesy of Florida Music Awards Hall of Fame, Wayne Koss.)

made as art
The Michael Braun Story

Michael Braun is a clothing designer who designed stage clothing for a number of local and national bands and artists including Jimi Hendrix, Sly & the Family Stone, Chicago, Sonny & Cher, Bob Dylan, the Temptations, the Allman Brothers Band, the Tropics, and many other late 1960s, 1970s, 1980s, and 1990s musical artists. (Courtesy of Bryan Kaufman and Michael Braun.)

Country music legend Mel Tillis was born in Tampa. Tillis attended the University of Florida, though he dropped out. In 1955, Tillis took a job with the Atlantic Coast Line Railroad in Tampa. Tillis moved to Nashville, Tennessee, to become a full-time songwriter. Tillis wrote "I'm Tired," which became a No. 3 country hit for Webb Pierce in 1957. Other Tillis hits included "Honky Tonk Song" and "Tupelo County Jail." Tillis eventually signed his own deal with Columbia Records and released "The Violet and a Rose" in 1958, which became his first Top 40 hit. His next single, "Sawmill," became a Top 25 hit. In 1969, Tillis released "These Lonely Hands of Mine" and "She'll Be Hanging Around Somewhere," which both became Top 10 country hits. In 1970, he reached the top five with "Heart Over Mind," which peaked at No. 3 on the hot country songs list. Tillis continued to record hit songs through the 1970s and 1980s. Tillis died of respiratory failure on November 19, 2017, in Ocala, Florida, at the age of 85. (Courtesy of Douglas Cifers, FMI Publishing.)

Five
THE MUSIC SCENE EXPLOSION
1980s–1990s

The Tampa Bay music scene exploded wide open in the 1980s. Paving the way were two Tampa Bay rock bands, Savatage (formerly Avatar) and Stranger. Both bands would eventually sign major label deals during the 1980s. This would open the doors for other bands as record labels started looking at Tampa Bay as a hotbed of talent, comparable to the Los Angeles music scene. Other local bands that would see major label deals during this time include Roxx Gang, the Hazies (formerly UROK), and Julliet.

Other prominent Tampa Bay bands who made a name for themselves during this time included Four in Legion, Blade, Multi Color House, Bleeding Hearts, Arazmo, the Damon Fowler Group, Deloris Telescope, Freaks Rule, DeeForce, Powersurge, Iced Earth, Noiz, Blackkout, Messiaxx, and Men From Earth, just to name a few.

Due to the overwhelming amount of talent in the area during this time, record companies, recording studios, and music venues started opening up everywhere in the area. Venues would have lines of people waiting outside to get in to listen to their favorite bands. Venues such as the Rock-it Club, ML Chasers, the Volley Club, Biarritz Nightclub, Alley Cats, Brass Mug, Killian's, and Bourbon Street were hugely popular. Local radio and television stations started featuring local bands routinely.

During this time, Tampa Bay gave birth to a new genre and style of music called death metal. Tampa Bay was producing most of the death metal bands, and the ones that were not from Tampa Bay started coming here to record in such studios as Morrisound Studios in Tampa. This would soon earn Tampa Bay the moniker of "the Birth Place of Death Metal."

Several awards shows started being held annually in the area to honor local artists, with the more well-known ones being the Bay Area Music Awards, Tampa Bay Music Awards, Tampa Bay Metal Awards, and the Florida Jammy Awards.

Popular local music magazines that went into publication at the time included *Jam Magazine*, *Thrust*, *Music Players*, and *Music Forum*.

As the mid-1990s rolled around, it seemed like nothing would slow down the music scene here in Tampa Bay.

Roxx Gang was a glam metal band formed in St. Petersburg in 1982. The band signed with Virgin Records in 1987, with a lineup consisting of Kevin Steele (vocals), Jeff Blanchard (guitar), Wade Hayes (guitar), Roby Strine (bass), and David Blackshire (drums). Their debut album, *Things You've Never Done Before*, was released in 1988, selling a quarter-million copies worldwide and spawning two singles: "No Easy Way Out" and "Scratch My Back." Roxx Gang would go through numerous lineup changes in the 1990s, resulting in the additions of Dallas Perkins (guitar), Andy James (drums), Tommy Weder (drums), Stacey Blades (guitar) Dorian Sage (bass), Jeff Vitolo (guitar), and Allen Brooks (bass). Roxx Gang would release several more albums before disbanding. The 2006 action-adventure video game *Saints Row* features two Roxx Gang songs, "Ball 'N Chain" and "No Easy Way Out." (Both, courtesy of Tampa Bay Music Scene Historical Society.)

Savatage was formed as Avatar in Tarpon Springs in 1979 before changing its name in 1983. Savatage's first two albums, *Sirens* (1983) and *The Dungeons Are Calling* (1984), were released on Par Records. In 1985, they signed a contract with Atlantic Records and released their third album, *Power of the Night*. Savatage has released a toal of 11 studio albums, 2 live albums, 4 compilations, and 3 EPs. Though originally consisting of Jon Oliva (lead vocals and keys), Criss Oliva (guitars and vocals), Keith Collins (bass and vocals), and Steve "Doc" Wacholz (drums), lineup changes had seen many other notable musicians join the band such as Johnny Lee Middleton, Chris Caffery, Zachary Stevens, Jeff Plate, and Al Pitrelli. In 1996, Savatage morphed into the highly successful Trans-Siberian Orchestra. Savatage's "Hall of the Mountain King" is featured in the 2006 action-adventure video game, Brütal Legend. (Both, courtesy of Tampa Bay Music Scene Historical Society.)

Guitarist Henry Paul moved to Temple Terrace as a young boy. At the age of 17, he started playing gigs at high school folk festivals as well as at the 18th String Coffee House and Music Emporium in Tampa. Paul joined the Outlaws in 1972. The Outlaws started playing clubs all around the Tampa area. Paul left the Outlaws in 1978 and formed the Henry Paul Band (pictured here). The band signed with Atlantic Records later that year and released *Grey Ghost*. The band's next album, *Feel the Heat* (1980), included three songs that went to No. 3 on the Billboard Bubbling Under the Hot 100 singles chart. Their third album, *Anytime* (1981), included the hit "Keeping Our Love Alive," No. 50 on the Billboard Hot 100 chart and No. 23 Billboard Top Tracks (mainstream rock tracks chart) in 1982. During this time, Paul started doing voiceover work for Tampa radio station 95ynf FM. The Henry Paul Band disbanded in 1983 when Paul reunited with the Outlaws. Paul left the Outlaws again in 1989 and formed a country band, BlackHawk, in 1991. (Courtesy of Henry Paul.)

Stranger is arguably one of the most famous bands to come out of Tampa Bay. Originally Named Lynxx and then Romeo before settling on Stranger, the band gained a fanatical following throughout Florida. Stranger was discovered by record producer Tom Werman and signed with Epic Records/CBS Records in 1981. The band released its self-titled debut album on April 18, 1982. The album contained the tracks "Swamp Woman" and "Jackie's So Bad," which both received considerable airplay on Florida radio, as well as many other markets throughout the United States. While in production of their second album, *No Rules*, Epic released the band from their contract. Stranger was offered a new deal with Atlantic Records but turned it down due to unfavorable clauses contained within the contract. During this time, Stranger toured heavily throughout Florida. Due to this, fans became familiar with the songs on the second album long before its 1989 release. Greg Billings left the band in 1996 to form Damn the Torpedoes. Stranger tried to continue with another singer but broke up for good shortly after. (Courtesy of Douglas Cifers, FMI Publishing.)

Ask anyone who was around the Tampa Bay music scene in the 1990s, and they will say that one of the most popular bands at that time was Cheeky Monkey. Cheeky Monkey was formed in 1992 by Rebecca Field (guitar), Andrea Campbell (vocals), Tina Stinson (guitar), Steve Embry (bass), and Jerry Balzano (drums). Later, band members would include Lee Pons, Nydia Lynn, Michael Dillon, and John Stepanik. Cheeky Monkey became hugely popular, playing all over the Tampa Bay area and opening for numerous major acts such as Quiet Riot, Joe Perry of Aerosmith, Warrant, and many more. The band would break up in 1999, with the members moving on to other popular acts. (Both, courtesy of Tampa Bay Music Scene Historical Society.)

Sean Phillips   Keith Sterling   Todd Plant   Oliver Hanson   Ralph Santolla

Eyewitness was formed in 1992 by guitarist Ralph Santolla and drummer Oliver Hanson. The band recruited Keith Sterling, Shawn Phillips, and Todd Plant to complete the lineup and rapidly became in demand on the Florida touring circuit. Pictured here is the original lineup in 1992; from left to right are Shawn Phillips, Keith "Sterling" Hancock, Todd Plant, Oliver Hanson, and Ralph Santolla. (Courtesy of Todd Plant.)

Eventually, both Sterling and Phillips left Eyewitness, and Steve Hodson and Michael Caruso would join. Eyewitness signed with UK record label Now & Then Records after executives heard some of the band's demos. The band released their self-titled debut album in 1995, which was produced by Scott Burns. Pictured here is Eyewitness after arriving at Heathrow Airport in London for the Gods Melodic Rock Festival in 1995. (Courtesy of Todd Plant.)

Following the release of their debut album in 1995, Eyewitness appeared at the Now & Then Records Gods 1995 concert, which took place at the Astoria 2 in London. Their follow-up album, *Messiah Complex*, was released but did not do as well as their debut release. Messiah Complex was only released in Japan. Hodson left the band around this time and was replaced with Manfred Binder. Soon after, the band changed their name, morphing into Millenium. Pictured above in London, from left to right are Eyewitness members Steve Hodson, Mike Caruso (rhythm guitar), Todd Plant, Oliver Hanson, and Ralph Santolla. Pictured below from left to right are Oliver Hanson, Ralph Santolla, Steve Hodson, and Todd Plant. (Both, courtesy of Todd Plant.)

Singer Todd Plant is a Tampa Native who attended Tampa's Plant High School. After graduating from high school, Plant spent some time in the US Navy before being honorably discharged. In 1992, Plant joined Tampa band Eyewitness as their lead singer, releasing two albums with the band. In 1996, the band morphed into Millenium. Millenium released three albums with Plant fronting the band. Eventually, Plant would leave Millenium to do solo work. Plant would go on to work with former members of the Doobie Brothers, Steely Dan, Chicago, Firefall, Blue Oyster Cult, Rick Derringer, Judas Priest, and the Bee Gees, as well as Eric Clapton's percussionist Joe Lala, Tom Petty and Rascals bassist Charlie Souza, and Jimi Hendrix and Santana drummer Buddy Miles. Though uncredited, Plant is the voice singing wrestling legend Hulk Hogan's "American Made" ring entrance song that played on both WCW and WWE television programs. Pictured here, Plant performs on stage at Tampa's legendary Rock-it Club in 1992. (Courtesy of Todd Plant.)

Triple Crown was a Tampa Bay band formed in 1987. The band consisted of, from left to right, Russ Bertolino, John Stepaniak, Link Detten, and Bill Webber. Triple Crown became an instant local success, performing weekly in area venues and nightclubs for the next six years. *Music Magazine* named Triple Crown one of "The Best of the Bay" in its July 29, 1989, issue. (Courtesy of Bill Webber.)

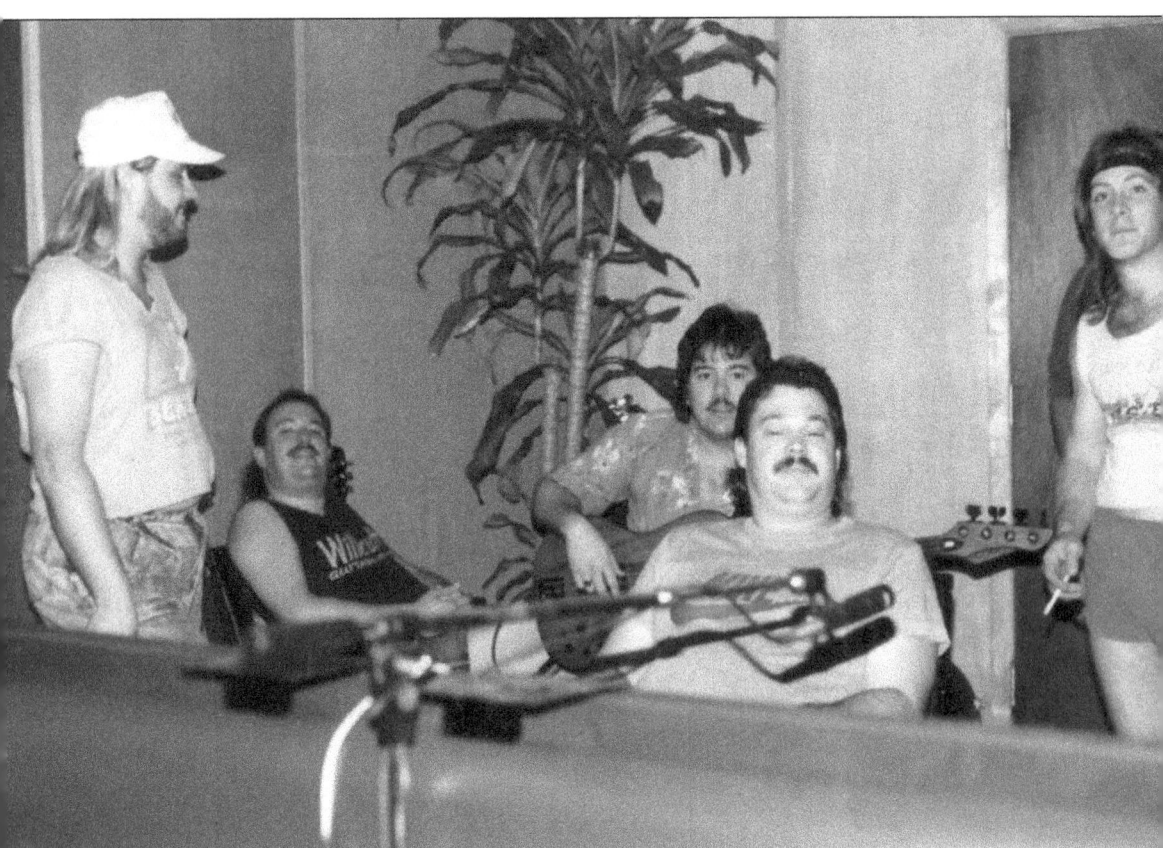

Triple Crown's six-song EP, *Baby Please*, was given a glowing review by *Players* magazine in its October 18, 1990, issue. In the review, the magazine called the release "very professional, with well-written and meticulously arranged songs." Pictured here in the recording studio are, from left to right, Link Detten, Bill Webber (seated), Russ Bertolino (seated), Robert Crosthwaite, and John Stepaniak. (Courtesy of Bill Webber.)

From the early 1980s to the late 1990s, Rocky Ruckman would front several memorable Tampa Bay bands. Among these bands were Monarch (1980–1982), Full Steam Eddy (1982–1983), Blanco (1983–1987), and Misspent Youth (1987–1988). However, the band that made the biggest impression, and the band that Ruckman became most remembered for, is Rocky Ruckman & the Beat Heathens. During the band's tenure, which lasted from 1988–1997, Rocky Ruckman & The Beat Heathens would consistently pack area venues with their huge following. The band released two recordings including a five-song EP early on, followed by their 1993 album, *It's a Scary World Out There*. Ruckman was presented with his official nomination into the Tampa Bay Music Hall of Fame on June 29, 2014. Ruckman passed away on April 16, 2015, at the age of 62. (Both, courtesy of Tampa Bay Music Scene Historical Society.)

Formed in Largo in 1981 as Zeke Leisure & the Casuals, Deloris Telescope originally consisted of Lee Steel on guitar, Dave Fairman on bass, Russ Hammock on drums, Bruce Batton on guitar, and Dale Fairman on keyboards and vocals. Following the departure of Dale Fairman, Zeke Leisure & the Casuals changed their name to Deloris Telescope. Momentum did not begin to build for the band until 1984, when Batton and Hammock left the band and were replaced by Kacy Ross (the Theatre Band) and André Belloice. Eventually, Ricky Wilcox would join the band and take over drum duties, helping to make Deloris Telescope a fixture on Tampa Bay's alternative-rock scene for nearly two decades. Eventually, the band would go on to win several music awards, appeared on radio, television, film, and recorded a string of highly successful albums. The band became a household name throughout Florida and will always be remembered as one of Tampa Bay's most popular bands of the 1980s and early 1990s. (Courtesy of Tampa Bay Music Scene Historical Society.)

Blackkout was formed in 1984 by Richard W. Elliott IV (vocals, guitars), Gale P. Morse (guitars), Eddie "Triad" Gayton (bass), and Jeff Patton (drums). The band released a seven-inch vinyl single "Fallout" in 1985. In 1988, the band hit the studio yet again, this time as a trio consisting of Richard Elliott IV, Jeffery Klaus, and Eddie "Triad" Gayton. One year later, the band released their full-length album *Ignorance of Man*. After 1990, the band consisted of Richard Elliott IV (Vocals, guitar, flute, bagpipes), Jerry Outlaw (vocals, guitars), Darren McFarland (bass), and Lee Gibson (drums). The band broke up shortly after, with certain members forming a new band called the Last Things. *Ignorance of Man* was rereleased in 2010 on the Greek label Arkeyn Steel. The rereleased album contained the original tracks from their 1985 release, as well as bonus material. (Both, courtesy of Bradley Davis, Tampa Bay Music Scene Historical Society.)

Messiaxx was a heavy metal band that formed in St. Petersburg in 1985 from the ashes of the band Noiz. The band's song "Island of Enchantress" was featured on the 1988 compilation album *Tampa Bay's Metal Mercenaries: The Invasion* (C-Me Records), which also featured other Tampa Bay metal bands such as Blackout, Oblivion, Keith Kollins Krunch, and Iced Earth. (Courtesy of Bradley Davis, Tampa Bay Music Scene Historical Society.)

From left to right are Lance Abair (the Continentals, the Impacs), Dennis Ballew, Kurt Curtis (author of *Florida's Famous and Forgotten*), Vic Waters (Vic Waters and the Entertainers), and Bobby Barnes at the St. Petersburg Coliseum during an event in 1993. This photograph was taken on the same day as the area was being hit by the "No Name Storm of '93." (Courtesy of Lance Abair.)

Little Jake Mitchell is an R&B singer of Cuban and Spanish descent from the Tampa Bay area. Singing since he was six years old, Mitchell has performed all over the United States and has made recordings for Impact Records, Newton Records, and his own label, Golden Hit Productions. In 1960, Mitchell's band Little Jake and the Blenders made history by becoming the first African American singing group to ever perform at the University of Florida's Gator Growl event held in Gainesville. The event's promoters had to install extra bleachers in the football field end zone to accommodate all the African Americans who were in attendance for the event. Aside from their performance, the group was also in the parade and was seen on the televised broadcast. Following their performance at Gator Growl, the group was booked solid for the next two years at the university's various sorority and fraternity houses. Mitchell has performed with T-Bone Walker, legendary Motown bassist James Jamerson, and Sarasota Slim. Pictured from left to right are Sarasota Slim and Mitchell at the Ringside Café in St. Petersburg in 1997. (Courtesy of Douglas Cifers, FMI Publishing.)

Rock violinist-singer Robby Steinhardt is best known for being the co-lead singer for Kansas from 1973 to 1982 and 1997 to 2006. Following his initial departure from Kansas, Steinhardt moved to Tampa and formed Steinhardt-Moon with guitarist Rick Moon (Stormbringer). During Steinhardt's tenure with Steinhardt-Moon, the band consisted of Robby Steinhardt (vocals and violin), Rick Moon (guitars and vocals), John Vasalakis (vocals), Eddie Pecchio (bass and vocals), John Zahner (keyboards and vocals), and Dana Newcomer (drums and percussion). The band released two albums, *Steinhardt-Moon* (1995) and *Moonshot* (1999). (Courtesy of Robbie Steinhardt.)

Formed in 1997, Millenium was a Tampa heavy metal band who released six albums, including *Millenium* (1997), *Angelfire* (1999 on Frontiers Records), *Hourglass* (2000), *The Best of . . . and More* (2004), *Jericho* (2004), and *Hourglass: The Complete Sessions* (2017). Pictured here in Fort Meyers in 1999 are Oliver Hanson (drums), Ralph Santolla (lead guitar), Todd Plant (vocals), Manfred Binder (bass), and Shane French (guitar). The band has also included Steve McKenna and Mark Prator. (Courtesy of Todd Plant.)

Wendy Rich formed the Soulshakers in 1991 after moving to the Tampa Bay area from Texas. The group quickly became one of Tampa Bay's most successful acts. Wendy & the Soulshakers garnered numerous awards for their high-energy blues-influenced rock; the band has performed with such greats as Edgar Winter, John Sebastian, Georgia Satellites, and Molly Hatchett. Wendy Rich headlined many Tampa Bay concert series such as The Point 102.5 FM's Ybor Rock 'N Blues Series, Tampa's Friday Extra Concerts, and the Hyde Park Music Series. In 2000 and 2004, Wendy Rich took a break from the Soulshakers to tour the United States and Europe as front person for Janis Joplin's band, Big Brother & the Holding Company. (Both, courtesy of Wendy Rich.)

Wendy Rich
This Time

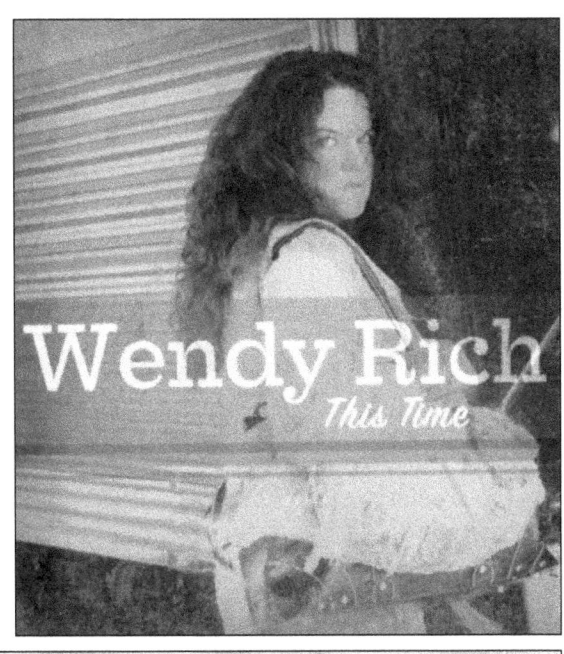

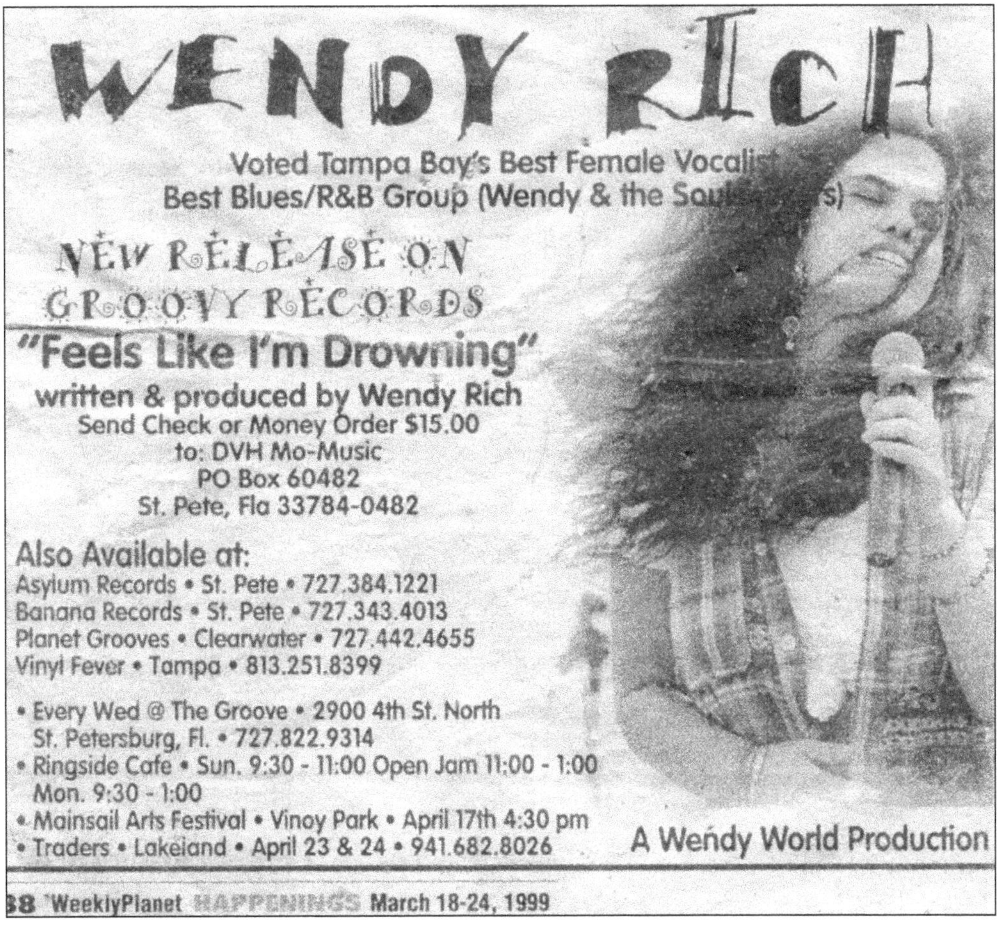
WENDY RICH
Voted Tampa Bay's Best Female Vocalist
Best Blues/R&B Group (Wendy & the Soulshakers)
NEW RELEASE ON
GROOVY RECORDS
"Feels Like I'm Drowning"
written & produced by Wendy Rich
Send Check or Money Order $15.00
to: DVH Mo-Music
PO Box 60482
St. Pete, Fla 33784-0482
Also Available at:
Asylum Records • St. Pete • 727.384.1221
Banana Records • St. Pete • 727.343.4013
Planet Grooves • Clearwater • 727.442.4655
Vinyl Fever • Tampa • 813.251.8399
• Every Wed @ The Groove • 2900 4th St. North
St. Petersburg, Fl. • 727.822.9314
• Ringside Cafe • Sun. 9:30 - 11:00 Open Jam 11:00 - 1:00
Mon. 9:30 - 1:00
• Mainsail Arts Festival • Vinoy Park • April 17th 4:30 pm
• Traders • Lakeland • April 23 & 24 • 941.682.8026
A Wendy World Production
38 WeeklyPlanet HAPPENINGS March 18-24, 1999

Though born in New Jersey, saxophonist-vocalist Eric Darius grew up in Tampa. Darius began his performing career at the age of 11, when he joined and toured with Sonny LaRosa and America's Youngest Jazz Band. At age 13, Darius left the youth band. With his father as his manager, Darius started appearing all over the Tampa Bay area with his own band, performing over 100 shows per year. During this time, Darius attended Howard W. Blake High School of the Performing Arts in Tampa and performed with the school's jazz band. At age 17, he released his first album independently. After high school, Darius attended the University of South Florida in Tampa, where he studied business and music. Darius joined the university's Jazztet and later signed his first recording contract with Higher Octave Music. (Both, courtesy of Eric Darius.)

No Tampa Bay recording studio has become more iconic than Morrisound Recording. Owned and operated by brothers Jim and Tom Morris, Morrisound Recording initially began in June 1981 as a mobile eight-track analog recording studio before opening their permanent studio in Temple Terrace in November 1981. Though the studio has always catered to all genres of music, Morrisound initially gained worldwide notoriety in the late 1980s and early 1990s as being responsible for the popularization of death metal, leading to Tampa Bay becoming known as "the Birthplace of Death Metal." Some of the more notable Tampa Bay bands to record albums at Morrisound include Savatage, Morbid Angel, Death, Control Denied, Obituary, Deicide, Iced Earth, Six Feet Under, Trans-Siberian Orchestra, Atheist, Kamelot, Crimson Glory, and Bleeding Hearts. Other major acts that have recorded at Morrisound include Destiny's Child, Seven Mary Three, and Warrant. (Courtesy of Tampa Bay Music Scene Historical Society.)

Kenny McGee is a veteran Tampa Bay singer-songwriter who is most known for his time as the lead singer of the 1990s glam band Julliet. Formed in Tampa Bay in the late 1980s, Julliet consisted of McGee (lead vocals), Jimmi DeLisi (guitars), Ty Westerhoff (bass), and Greg Pecka (drums). The band was hugely popular in Florida before relocating to Los Angeles, signing with Enigma/Capitol Records and releasing their debut self-titled album in 1990. Eventually, McGee would return to Florida, where he formed the band Heartless, followed by the band Lefty. After performing with both Heartless and Lefty, McGee would embark on his solo career. As a solo artist, McGee released several albums, including *Kenny McGee and Lefty* (1997), *Roughcuts Demos* (2001), *Kenny McGee's Disease* (2001), *Kenny McGee* (2002), *Heartless Daze Volume 1* (2009), *Heartless Daze Volume 2* (2009), and *Legends Roll* (2012). McGee would also reunite with Julliet in the 2000s to release two more albums, including *Psycho Boyfriend* (2004) and *Passion* (2006). (Courtesy of Tampa Bay Music Scene Historical Society.)

Known as "Tampa's Frank Zappa," Ray "Rayzilla" Villadonga was a Tampa Bay singer-songwriter, bassist, and radio show host. Villadonga was born and raised in Ybor City and was a third-generation Floridian. Villadonga started playing guitar and writing songs at age 12. While attending Tampa Catholic High School, Villadonga played flute in the school's band. After graduating high school, Villadonga attended the University of South Florida's School of Music. (Courtesy of the *Tampa Bay Times*.)

Villadonga went to work for Tampa's WMNF radio in 1986. He would spend 30 years at WMNF, hosting radio shows such as Sonic Irritations and Step Outside. Villadonga played in many local bands and released several albums throughout his career. One of those bands was the World Fusion Band (pictured here after Villadonga's death in 2017), which played a contemporary style of music with Indian and Eastern influences. (Courtesy of WMNF Community Radio.)

The Mod Squad was formed in 1987 by Joey Donovan and Karen Deal. Deal graduated from Tampa Catholic High School in 1971 and was the daughter of Arch Deal, a newscaster for WFLA. Prior to forming the Mod Squad, Deal was already performing with another Tampa Bay–area band, the Johnny Charro Review. With Donovan on guitar and Deal on bass and keyboards, the two eventually recruited Rodger Stephan on drums to complete the Mod Squad. Pictured here in 1990, the trio kept busy for the first two years. Deal met Jefferson Airplane singer Marty Balin while the Mod Squad was opening for Balin's new band, the Marty Balin Band. Deal and Balin started seeing each other and eventually got married. After leaving the Mod Squad, Deal moved to California with Balin and eventually went on tour with the newly formed Jefferson Airplane. The Mod Squad's final gig was at Skipper's Smokehouse's anniversary celebration just seven weeks before Deal's death in 2010. (Courtesy of Joey Donovan.)

Six
THE NEW MILLENNIUM
2000s–2010s

The music industry, on the whole, took a drastic turn by the time 2000 came along, and it affected the Tampa Bay music scene. Much like Tampa Bay gave birth to death metal in the 1980s, Seattle, Washington, had given birth to grunge. By this point, grunge rock had managed to cement their foundation strongly into the national music scene, and the record industry started taking note. By the late 1990s, the record industry was focusing their attention on Seattle, no longer interested in the bands or musical style that Tampa Bay had to offer.

The local music scene started to slow down. Local venues started booking only cover bands, and many popular venues started to close down. As a result, fans became increasingly uninterested in the local live music scene.

With the music scene stagnating, local music publications went out of business, mainstream media stopped reporting on the local scene, and recording studios started shutting down. Management and promotion companies started shutting down or relocating to other markets outside of the Tampa Bay area.

Even with the local scene being a shell of itself, there were still original bands and artists that would occasionally form and gain a popular following. Some of these acts included Diamond Gray, 1404, Amber Lynn Nicol, Stonegrey, Geri X, Wikkid, 20 Shades, ZigZag America, and many more.

By 2010, many had long forgotten what the Tampa Bay music scene was once like. Those who remembered the glory days would speculate and come up with theories as to what happened to cause the local music scene to take a dramatic turn and die out. Some theories are that the scene simply imploded due to oversaturation and overexposure.

Thanks to nonprofit organizations such as the Tampa Bay Music Hall of Fame (founded in the early 2000s) and the Tampa Bay Music Scene Historical Society (founded in 2012), the Tampa Bay's musical history and contributions to the national music scene can be researched, honored, and remembered for all time.

Born and raised in Tampa Bay, Tedd Webb is a semiretired radio personality who has manned the microphone for such Tampa Bay radio stations as Newsradio 970 WFLA, WALT, WFSO, WLCY, WDAE, WNSI, WPLP, and WRBQ Q-105 FM. In addition to being one of the most recognized radio personalities in Tampa Bay, Webb also hosted *Sports Rap*, which aired for eight years on WFTS Channel 28. (Courtesy of Premier Studios.)

Webb is also a Tampa Bay music scene historian. His website is full of old photographs and biographies of 1960s-era Tampa Bay bands, which he has compiled throughout the years. Webb has won numerous awards for his work, including the "Communicator of the Year" award from Toastmasters International, and the "2001 Hispanic Heritage Man of the Year in Media" award. Webb was inducted into the Jefferson High School Hall of Fame in 2002. (Courtesy of Premier Studios.)

Tampa Bay rock band Wikkid was formed in 2010 by Tim Knisely, Jay Diesel, David Seifert, and Brad Davis. With their high-energy stage presence, Wikkid quickly gained momentum and built up a huge fan base in the Tampa Bay area. The year 2011 saw the departure of Davis and Seifert, replaced by Owen Law and Matt Lupori. Wikkid managed to collect several local awards and honors. In 2011, Seifert and Knisely both received individual endorsement deals from Spawn Guitars. That same year, drummer Jay Diesel won the "Sexiest Drummer of 2011" award, as well as the "Sexiest Musician of 2011," award at the 2011 KAM-BABS Sexiest Musicians of Tampa Bay Awards Ceremony in Tampa. In 2012, Wikkid won the award for "TBMN Favorite Rock Band of 2011" at the fourth annual TBMN Music Awards, presented by the Tampa Bay Music Network. Jay Diesel also won the "*Mayhem Magazine* Drummer of the Year" award at the same event. Wikkid disbanded in March 2013 following Knisely's departure in December 2012. Wikkid reformed in 2017, with Knisely rejoining the band. (Both, courtesy of Keith Wilkins, the *St. Petersburg Examiner*, KAM Music Publishing.)

Tommy Roxx & Big Deal is a Southern rock band formed in Clearwater in 2000. Aside from Roxx (lead vocals) himself, the band has also featured many local musicians throughout the years, including Tony Jones (guitar and vocals), Dave Bugee (guitar and vocals), Rocky Diamond (guitar and vocals), Brian Jeffries (guitar), John Varr (guitar), Peter Kane (keyboards), Dave Stevenson (bass and vocals), Brian "Bam Bam" Bradford (drums), and Rob Bird (drums). Tommy Roxx & Big Deal released their debut album, *Freedom Isn't Free*, in 2013. The album featured songs such as "Freedom Isn't Free," "I Cried Myself to Sleep," "I Wanna Do Everything," "Little Girl o' Mine," "Or What?!?," "Two Girls Kissin'," "Unleash the Freak," "Who in the Hell," and "You Were the One." Pictured here, Tommy Roxx & Big Deal perform live at the L.A. Hangout in Lutz. (Both, courtesy of Keith Wilkins, the *St. Petersburg Examiner*, KAM Music Publishing.)

Primal Shift is a Tampa Bay hard rock duo that formed in the early 2010s. The duo consists of Leslie Redman (guitars, drums, bass, vocals, and keyboards, on the left) and April Davis (lead vocals). Though Primal Shift was Davis's first band, Redman had played in numerous bands in the Tampa Bay area prior to Primal Shift. Primal Shift released their debut seven-song EP, *Disturbing Element*, in 2014. (Courtesy of Leslie Redman and April Davis.)

Demented Truth is a metal band consisting of Danny Shaner (vocals), Mark Denman (guitar), Craig Daniels (bass), and Vance West (drums). Formed in Tampa in 2013, Demented Truth played their first club show in front of 75 people after being together only three weeks. Within two months, they were opening for national acts. (Courtesy of the *St. Petersburg Examiner*, KAM Music Publishing.)

The band 1404 was a Tampa Bay progressive hard rock band that was popular in the early 2000s. Formed in 1999, the band consisted of April Wharton (lead vocals), Mike McCann (lead guitar), Scott Lewis Chase (guitar), Brad Davis (bass), Glenn Laubaugh (keyboards), and Rich Lesniak (drums). They released their self-titled album in 2001, which was recorded at ESP Studios in Pinellas Park. During the recording of the album, Lesniak left the band. At the time, Lesniak was the airport manager at the St. Petersburg downtown airport. Since there was so much marijuana being smoked around the band, Lesniak had to quit the band since he was under FAA supervision. Lesniak was replaced on the drums by Ricky Teague. Shortly after the release of the album, Wharton left the band and was replaced by Chuck Zang. The band broke up in 2003. (Both, courtesy of Bradley Davis, Tampa Bay Music Scene Historical Society.)

Two-time Grammy Award–nominated saxophonist, vocalist, author, and national trustee for the National Academy of Recording Arts and Sciences, Mindi Abair was born in St. Petersburg. Mindi's father is saxophonist Lance Abair, who played in numerous Tampa Bay bands in the 1960s and 1970s, including the Continentals, the Impacs, and Vic Waters and the Entertainers. After graduated magna cum laude from the Berklee College of Music in Boston, Mindi moved to Los Angeles in 1991 and eventually started touring with such artists as John Tesh, Adam Sandler, Bobby Lyle, Jonathan Butler, and the Backstreet Boys. Eventually, Mindi went out on her own to become a high-profile recording artist. In 2007, Mindi took over as host on the nationally syndicated radio program *Chill with Chris Botti*. The name changed to *Chill with Mindi Abair*, and she hosted the show until 2015. (Courtesy of Lance Abair.)

In 2003, Mindi Abair signed with Verve/GRP Records and released her album *It Just Happens That Way*, which peaked at No. 7 on the Billboard Contemporary Jazz chart. The album spawned a single, "Lucy's," which played on smooth jazz stations where it stayed at number one on the charts for eight straight weeks, tying a record for consecutive weeks at No. 1. Her 2006 album, *Life Less Ordinary*, peaked at No. 1 on the Billboard Contemporary Jazz chart, where it remained in the top 20 for 45 weeks. Her songs "True Blue" and "Bloom" hit No. 1. Abair released *Hi-Fi Stereo* in 2010, which peaked at No. 6 on the Billboard Jazz Albums chart and spawned the No. 1 hit "Be Beautiful." In 2014, Abair released *Wild Heart*, which debuted at No. 1 on the Billboard Jazz chart. The record was nominated for Best Contemporary Instrumental Album in the 2015 Grammy Awards. (Courtesy of Lance Abair.)

The Unknown was a local rock band consisting of Bruce Miller on vocals, Joe Stephens on guitar and vocals, Bradley Davis on bass and vocals, and Marty Lindemann on drums and vocals. The Unknown performed all over the area, including places like Baby Boomerz in Seminole. (Courtesy of Bradley Davis, Tampa Bay Music Scene Historical Society.)

Singer-songwriter Autumn June broke into the Tampa Bay music scene in early 2014 after getting her start by playing at open jams throughout Pinellas County. June recorded her first single, "My Favorite Window," while on tour in Europe in 2017. She released her second single, "Release Me," later that same year. (Courtesy of Tampa Bay Music Scene Historical Society.)

Muphin Chuckrs are an alternative rock band that formed in Palmetto, Florida, in 1999. The band consists of Dustin White (lead vocals and guitar), Dan Edwards (guitar), Nate Reid (bass), and Zach Phillipsare (drums). The band quickly grew a huge following while performing on the local music scene, especially with the younger crowd. Muphin Chuckrs has released a total of 10 albums since its formation in 1999. Albums include *Titillating Duo* (2001), *For the Good of Mankind* (2003), *Straight from Hell* (2004), *Good Shit* (2004), *Greed* (2005), *Chill* (2006), *House Party Heroes* (2008), *Feedback Sux!* (2009), *From Life to Paper* (2010), and *How It Feels to Be Human* (2014). The band is pictured here performing at the Wildstock concert, which took place in Wimauma, Florida, in 2011. The daylong concert was put on by KAM-BABS Promotions in order to help raise money for Elmira's Wildlife Sanctuary. (Courtesy of Keith Wilkins, the *St. Petersburg Examiner*, KAM Music Publishing.)

Legendary promoter Anthony "Tony" Michaelides (left) and Keith Wilkins (right), pictured with singer-songwriter Amber Lynn Nicol (center), are at Nicol's CD release party for Nicol's 2012 album *Broader Horizons*. The event took place at the Ale & the Witch in downtown St. Petersburg on December 15, 2012. *Broader Horizons* was Nicol's second studio album, released on her own label, Jerzy Girl Music. (Courtesy of Kayla Wilkins, the *St. Petersburg Examiner*, KAM Music Publishing.)

Tampa Bay singer-songwriter Amber Lynn Nicol signs copies of her 2012 album, *Broader Horizons*, at a CD Release party that was held at the Ale & the Witch in downtown St. Petersburg on December 15, 2012. Nicol has released six studio albums, including *Beach Day* (2011), *Broader Horizons* (2012), *SEVEN* (2014), *Painted Fish* (2015), *The Bedroom Sessions* (2015), and *Endless Summer* (2016). (Courtesy of Keith Wilkins, he *St. Petersburg Examiner*, KAM Music Publishing.)

Pictured here is New Port Richey rock band ZigZag America following a December 9, 2012, performance at the Lucky Deuce in St. Petersburg. ZigZag America was originally formed in 1993 by singer Jimmy Starr and guitarist Mikk Tabakovic as ZigZag. After issues with various band members, ZigZag disbanded a year later in 1994. Starr and Tabakovic reformed the band in 2010 with a new lineup in 2011 consisting of Starr (lead vocals), Tabakovic (guitar), Jake Schaffer (bass), and Beau Garrow (drums). ZigZag soon changed its name to ZigZag America due to another band having the same name. Garrow left the band in 2012 and was replaced by Bobby Walker in 2013. Walker left the band later that year and was replaced by Chad Henderson. Henderson was the boyfriend of Dina Mead, ZigZag America's manager. The band released their debut album *.com* that same year in 2013. The band broke up in 2014 due to tension between some of the band members and their manager. Starr, Tabakovic, and Schaeffer later formed a new band together. (Courtesy of Keith Wilkins, the *St. Petersburg Examiner*, KAM Music Publishing.)

Tampa Bay hard rock band Rockstarr Bentley is pictured here performing at the 2014 Seminole Music & Sound Customer Appreciation party in Seminole. By this point, in 2014, Rockstarrr Bentley had exploded onto the local scene. The band released their first single, "Bigger," in 2012. In 2013, the band released their debut album titled *Trust in Rock*. Around this time, *Creative Loafing* magazine featured the band on its cover as well. Rockstarr Bentley has gone through a few lineup changes, featuring such musicians as Rocky Bentley, Kayla Johnson, Andrew Shaw, Gary Simonelli, Kei Alexander Bland, Michael Kiss, Lady J., and DeeJay Imminent. The band has performed with Anvil, Thin Lizzy, Uncrowned, Blackstar Whiskey, LuvDogs, and members of Savatage. Rockstarr Bentley has raised money for various charities, including the Wounded Warrior Project and the Breast Cancer Research Foundation. (Courtesy of Keith Wilkins, the *St. Petersburg Examiner*, KAM Music Publishing.)

Diamond Gray was formed in 1992 by guitarist Rocky Diamond and vocalist Danny Gray. Throughout their 20-year tenure, the band would go through several musical styles, including country, Southern rock, and hard rock. During that time, they would also go through several lineup changes. Some of the more notable members of the band included Dennis Daley, Todd Dyer, Tony King, Doug Lipps, Mike Townsend, Kevin Rothney, Brian Bradford, Michael J. Allen, Jeff Scott, David Runion, Mark Welsh, and Chris Krause, just to name a few. The band released three albums, including *Live to Play . . . Play to Live* (1997), *For You* (2002), and *Sound* (2011). In 2012, The title track to *Sound* captured the No. 13 position on the WMTB "Top 100 Songs of 2011" list. Diamond Gray officially broke up in 2013. (Above, courtesy of Rocky Diamond; below, courtesy of Keith Wilkins, Tampa Bay Music Scene Historical Society, KAM Music Publishing.)

Decepcion was a metal band formed in the Tampa Bay area in 2004. Managed by Dina Mead of Bay Area Band Source, the band consisted of Matt Morris (lead vocals, 2004–2010), Chuck Zang (lead vocals, 2010), Eileen Hensler (lead vocals, 2010–2011), Lance Balch (guitars and vocals, 2004–2011), Dave Sampson (bass and vocals, 2006–2011), and Jeremy Strait (drums, 2004–2011). Decepcion released one album, titled *Down South Cottonmouth*. The band officially broke up in 2011. Balch went on to play in Black Rose and the Luv Dogz, and Strait and Sampson went on to play in My Identity. Balch, Sampson, and Strait would do occasional performances as a three-piece under the Decepcion name. (Both, courtesy of Keith Wilkins, the *St. Petersburg Examiner*, KAM Music Publishing.)

Caroline Kole began her career as "Suite" Caroline, playing the beach bars in her hometown of Clearwater Beach, as well as gigs in Plant City at the young age of 10. After playing several recurring shows at the annual Strawberry Festival at the Florida State Fairgrounds in Plant City, Kole formed a backup band and moved to Nashville, Tennessee. Shortly after, country music icon Reba McEntire discovered Kole during one of her performances at the legendary Bluebird Café. McEntire signed Kole to a management deal with Starstruck Entertainment, and a publishing deal with Sony/ATV Music Publishing. Kole would go on to tour with McEntire, helping to propel the young singer's career. More recently, Kole has achieved a Top 30 album on iTunes, two No. 1 music videos on CMT, and features on SiriusXM. (Courtesy of Tampa Bay Music Scene Historical Society.)

Drummer Jerry LeBloch played with many bands during the 1960s–2010s, including Justice Myles, the Frost, Wayne Cochran and the C.C. Riders, the Platters, and many more. He played drums for Rare Earth, touring the world with the band from 1985 through 1990. LeBloch is A member of both the Michigan Rock Hall of Fame, and the Motown Records' Hall of Fame. In the early 2010s, LeBloch moved to Gulfport, Florida, and formed the Jerry LeBloch Band. The band played gigs all over the local music scene, and LeBloch made appearances on several local radio stations. LeBloch passed away from cancer on August 25, 2015. Pictured here, LeBloch performs at a benefit concert organized by KAM-BABS Promotions and held at the historic Porpoise Pub in Seminole on July 7, 2013. (Both, courtesy of Keith Wilkins, the *St. Petersburg Examiner*, KAM Music Publishing.)

Neal Nachman (left) and Keith Wilkins (right) are on the red carpet at the 2014 Talkie Awards held at the Tampa Picture Show in Tampa on April 4, 2014. Nachman and Wilkins appeared at the show to co-present the award for "Best Music Radio Show" live onstage. Nachman is the publisher of Tampa's *Full Access Magazine*. Wilkins, at the time, was a columnist for *Full Access Magazine*, the *St. Petersburg Examiner*, as well as the original cover-story writer for *Mayhem Magazine*. In addition, Wilkins has written over 600 articles for numerous other newspapers and magazines in the United States and United Kingdom. Wilkins was also an on-air interviewer on Tampa's WPRN 102.1 FM, the founder of the Tampa Bay Music Scene Historical Society, cofounder of KAM-BABS Promotions, and former contract songwriter. (Courtesy of Keith Wilkins, Tampa Bay Music Scene Historical Society, KAM Music Publishing.)

Formed in 2008, Save the Radio is a Tampa Bay alternative rock band that has consisted of Shawn Scheller, Mike MacKewice, Michael J. Marino, T.L. Jentgens, and Tony Rook. In May 2013, Save the Radio was signed to TazBull Records and released a five-song EP. Their single, "Add It Up," was released in January 2014 and peaked at No. 37 in April on the Billboard indicator charts, receiving airplay in over 25 markets. Aside from performing all over the Tampa Bay area, the band has toured throughout the United States. Pictured here are members of the band recording songs at Clear Track Recording Studios in Downtown Clearwater on July 11, 2014. (Both, courtesy of the *St. Petersburg Examiner*, KAM Music Publishing.)

Kole Kruger is a singer-songwriter from the Tampa Bay area who has played in several local and national bands, including Kole and Shadows Down. Kole features Kole Kruger (lead vocals), Mike Narcia (guitar), Dave Runion (bass), Ted Fillhart (keys), and Rob Knesz (drums). Kole has released several albums, including *God Is in the Music* (2006) and *Songs of Summer* (2009). (Courtesy of Tampa Bay Music Scene Historical Society.)

Tampa Bay syndicated music columnist Keith Wilkins (right) is pictured with rock legend Eddie Money (left) at the State Theatre in downtown St. Petersburg following one of Money's concerts in 2011. Wilkins was interviewing Money for his "St. Petersburg Live Music Bar Scene" column, which was published by the *Examiner*. (Courtesy of Keith Wilkins, the *St. Petersburg Examiner*, KAM Music Publishing.)

A winner of numerous awards, Ellie Lee is a Tampa Bay blues guitarist-singer-songwriter whose guitar virtuosity has been compared to Stevie Ray Vaughan, Gary Moore, and Jimi Hendrix. Aside from being a staple of the Tampa Bay music scene, Ellie Lee has also toured all throughout the southern United States. Though she has played in a variety of rock, blues, funk, and show bands throughout the years, she is best known in the Tampa Bay area for fronting the band Ellie Lee & Blues Fury. Ellie Lee & Blues Fury have released numerous albums, including *When the Night Train Comes* (2009), *Rhythm of the Blues* (2010), *My Time Now* (2010), *Day Late Dollar Short* (2012), and *Hybrid* (2016). Her band has consisted of area musicians such as Mike Biscutti, John Sipher, Jerry Hale, Dan Dial, Steve McCormack, and many others. (Courtesy of Tampa Bay Music Scene Historical Society.)

Paula Aubert is a singer-songwriter based out of the Tampa Bay area. Aubert was born and raised in the north woods of Minnesota, where she grew up in a very musical household. She started out performing in her high school choir, honing her vocal talents. Aubert took an interest in lyric writing at a young age. Though she tried to learn how to play guitar off and on in her younger years, Aubert did not start learning to play seriously until she was 21 years of age, shortly after giving birth to her daughter. As a single mother, a career in music seemed unlikely for her. With a sense of determination, Aubert sat in her tiny apartment for an entire winter and learned how to play guitar. Aubert released her album *Purdy Wings* in 2013. (Both, courtesy of Tampa Bay Music Scene Historical Society.)

Earl "the Pearl" Bucko (left) was a blues harmonica player who played in numerous Tampa Bay area bands beginning in the mid-1980s. These bands included Redhouse, the Charlie Morris Band, Lazy Boy and the Rockers, Cross Bayou Blues Band, and Honeyboy. Bucko owned Pearl Custom Harmonicas, where he built custom harmonicas for area blues musicians such as Rod Piazza, Mark Hummel, T.C. Carr, and Jason Ricci. In the 2010s, Bucko opened his own recording studio called SackOwoe Studios. SackOwoe Recording Studios has recorded projects for the Tampa Bay Ray's baseball team, the Trust Band, and the Crossroads Band. In 2004, Bucko formed the SackOwoe Blues Band with Steve Griggs (lead guitar), Jeff Avrin (bass), Tom Staley (drums), and himself on harmonica. Bucko is pictured here with Jerry LeBloch (right) at a benefit concert held for LeBloch in 2013 at the historic Porpoise Pub in Seminole. (Courtesy of Keith Wilkins, the *St. Petersburg Examiner*, KAM Music Publishing.)

Pictured here from left to right are Keith Wilkins, national recording artist Kole Kruger (Kole), and Dina Mead outside of Cusos in Indian Rocks Beach following a Kole show in 2012. At the time, Wilkins and Mead operated KAM-BABS Promotions, a promotions company that organized concerts, award shows, roasts, and radio shows throughout the Tampa Bay area. The main focus of KAM-BABS Promotions was to promote original Tampa Bay bands and artists during a time when mainly only cover bands were getting promoted in the local scene. KAM-BABS Promotions were mainly known for their monthly AMPD (Area Musicians Promoting Diversity) concert showcases that they held at the historic Porpoise Pub from 2013 to 2015, which featured both local and national original bands and artists. KAM-BABS Promotions ceased operations in September 2015. They held their last show at the Porpoise Pub just three weeks before it was destroyed by a fire. (Courtesy of Anna Tenpenny Photography, Tampa Bay Music Scene Historical Society.)

Craven Moorehead was a radio personality in the Tampa Bay area, operating from the 1990s until his death in 2019. Moorehead owned and operated WPRN 102.1 FM, "the party pirate." During the 2010s, WPRN broadcasted out of the Radio Bar and Grill, located next to Busch Gardens at 2806 East Busch Boulevard in Tampa. WPRN devoted blocks of airtime to playing original local music. Through KAM-BABS Promotions, the bar and grill also booked original local bands. In 2013, both the radio station and bar were severely damaged after a homemade bomb exploded in the building. Though the building was soon rebuilt, the bar closed about a year later, and WPRN relocated to Plant City. (Both, courtesy of Tampa Bay Music Scene Historical Society.)

Formed in St. Petersburg, the Mojo Gurus is a blues-rock band that morphed out of the ashes of the highly successful 1980s–1990s glam-rock band Roxx Gang, consisting of Kevin Steele (lead vocals and harmonica), Doc Lovett (guitar and vocals), Vinnie Granese (bass and vocals) and Sean Doyle (drums and vocals), the Mojo Gurus have toured throughout the United States as both headliner and the supporting act for bands such as David Allan Coe, Joe Perry, and Johnny Winter. The band has released several albums, including *Hot Damn!* (2004), *Shakin' In the Barn* (2005), *Let's Get Lit with . . . the Mojo Gurus* (2009), *Who Asked Ya?* (2014), and *Gone* (2017). The band's 2009 music video for "I Can't Stand to Hear That Song Again" was filmed at Dave's Aqua Lounge, a music venue that used to be located off of Gandy Boulevard in St. Petersburg. (Courtesy of Tampa Bay Music Scene Historical Society.)

Rebecca Field is a Tampa Bay guitarist and singer-songwriter who has been a veteran of the local music scene for over 30 years. Though Field has performed in countless local bands, the first band of Field's to gain major popularity was Cheeky Monkey in the 1990s. Cheeky Monkey consisted of Angie Campbell (lead vocals), Field (guitar and vocals), Lee Pons (bass and vocals), and Tom McCowan (drums). Mike Dillon, Juan Berrios, and others would also join the band during various incarnations. Field's second most popular band was Undercover Betty, a rock band formed in 2012 that consisted of Field (lead vocals and guitar), Connie Bonds (bass and vocals), Kana Leimbech (drums), and Carol Sarao (keyboards), who joined in 2014. Undercover Betty released a self-titled debut album in 2014. Field is pictured here performing at Livestock, a benefit concert that took place in Wimauma, Florida, in 2011. The day-long concert was put on by KAM-BABS Promotions, in order to help raise money for Elmira's Wildlife Sanctuary. (Courtesy of Keith Wilkins, the *St. Petersburg Examiner*, KAM Music Publishing.)

Lee Pons is a Tampa Bay singer-songwriter-bassist-keyboardist that has played in various local rock and blues bands for over 30 years. By the age of 16, Pons was already performing in clubs. Pons attended and graduated from the Juilliard School of Music, where he earned two degrees. After leaving Cheeky Monkey in 1999, Pons would become a popular blues musician. Pons won the *Creative Loafing* "Best of the Bay" award for Best Local Blues Artist in 2009. Pons also became a semifinalist in The Blues Foundation's Annual International Blues Challenge in 2010 and 2011. Pons released three solo albums, including *Big Boogie Voodoo* (2010), *Togged to the Bricks* (2012), and *After the Rain* (2018). Pons was inducted into the Blues Hall of Fame in 2016. Aside from his solo career and time in Cheeky Monkey, Pons also played in Buddy King's Shotgun Junkies. (Courtesy of Lee Pons, Tampa Bay Music Scene Historical Society.)

Born in Sarasota in 2000, Kei Alexander Bland (pictured second from the left) is a multi-instrumentalist child-prodigy who has mainly performed as the drummer in several popular Tampa Bay Bands. Bland made his first public appearance on stage in 2006 at the age of six and started playing local jams at age nine. At age 12, he was featured in DRUM! magazine. Bland formed the band 4Ever Endeavour (pictured here) in 2013. In 2014, Bland joined the band Avenging Benji. One year later, he enrolled in the Berklee College of Music, studying for his master's certification in music business. Kei has performed with Rick Derringer, Chris Anderson (the Outlaws), Mike Kach (Dickey Betts and Great Southern and Molly Hatchett), Tracey Austin (Bad Company), Paul Duffy (the Commitments), Michael Allman, Jeff Carlise (38 Special), Bert Englesman (the Allman Brothers), Frankie Lombardi (Dickey Betts and Great Southern), Phill Stokes (Pure Prairie League), Rhino Reinhardt (Iron Butterfly and Captain Beyond), Dave Flett (Thin Lizzy and Manfred Mann), and countless others. (Courtesy of Kei Alexander Bland, the St. Petersburg Examiner, KAM Music Publishing.)

Born in Chicago in 1957, blues musician Steve Arvey has been based out of the Tampa Bay area for years. Arvey got his start working as a sideman in Chicago during the late 1970s, before moving to Gainesville, Florida, to attend college. Though Arvey returned to Chicago after college, he moved back to the Sarasota area of Florida in 2007. Arvey signed with Warner Bros. International in 2005. In 2012, Arvey formed the Delta Swamp Rats, a Tampa Bay band with a Mississippi Delta Funk Sound. Throughout his career, Arvey has released numerous albums, toured all over the world, and has played with notable blues musicians such as Hubert Sumlin, Jimmy Rogers, Big Smokey Smothers, Homesick James, Andrew Brown, Lefty Dizz, Big Moose Walker, BB Big Voice Odum, Detroit Jr., Lovie Lee, Carey Bell, Big Jack Johnson, Sam Carr, Frank Frost, Lester Davenport. Eddie Taylor, Sam Lay, Eddie Clearwater, Sugar Blue, Abb Locke, Hip Linkchain, Sammy Lawhorn, Junior Wells, and Sammy Fender. (Courtesy of Tampa Bay Music Scene Historical Society.)

Back in 2009, the City of St. Petersburg was looking to adopt an official city song. In November of that year, the city held an online vote to choose a song, resulting in nearly 13,000 people casting their votes. The winning song was "Carry Me Back to St. Petersburg," written and performed by Charlie Souza. The song received 5,553 votes, approximately 43 percent of the votes cast. A Tampa Bay native, Souza has been a member of several Tampa Bay–area bands since the 1960s, including the Tropics, White Witch, Tom Petty's Mudcrutch, and many more. "Carry Me Back to St. Petersburg" was written from his own personal experiences. After moving to Los Angeles while in his 20s, Souza eventually got homesick. After experiencing an earthquake while living in California, Souza decided it was time to move back to his hometown of Tampa Bay, hence the title, "Carry Me Back to St. Petersburg." (Courtesy of Sue Michelson.)

Raised in Tampa, Janelle Sadler got her start performing in St. Petersburg beach clubs in the 1980s. Before long, she would make a name for herself in the Florida music scene, winning several local music awards. Sadler moved to Los Angeles in 1991 and started touring as a backup singer for Donny Osmond. She has appeared on *The Tonight Show with Jay Leno*, *The Rosie Show*, *The Today Show*, and has sung for the television series *Brothers and Sisters* and *Smallville*. In 2015, Sadler and her husband, Robin Swenson (pictured here with Sadler), who was a Los Angeles session player, toured and recorded with Frankie Valli & the Four Seasons and Air Supply and Chuck Negron, formerly of Three Dog Night, played keyboards and cowrote some of Janelle's records. The couple moved back to Florida, where they still perform regularly in the Tampa Bay area. (Both, courtesy of Robin Swenson and Janelle Sadler.)

Johnny Green (pictured right) was a Tampa Bay–area promoter whose first concert took place in Orlando and featured Jeff Beck on the bill. Green would go on to produce many shows throughout the Tampa Bay area, including the Taste of Pinellas events in St. Petersburg at Vinoy Park. Green is pictured here with Robin Zander (pictured left) of Cheap Trick. Zander has been a longtime resident of Safety Harbor. This photograph was taken at the Capitol Theatre in Clearwater on September 8, 2018. Zander was performing in a trio with his son Robin Taylor Zandor and his daughter Robin Sailor Zandor. (Courtesy of Lyn Orns and Amber Lynn Nicole.)

Visit us at
arcadiapublishing.com

www.ingramcontent.com/pod-product-compliance
Lightning Source LLC
Chambersburg PA
CBHW060938170426
43194CB00027B/2994